Fishing

A Handbook for Beginners

Benno Sigloch

Picture credits:

Werner Berens (pp. 38, 72, 74, 75, 76, 77), Franz Bindl (ASV Bodenwöhr) (p. 26 b), Frank Brodrecht (p. 93), Michael Dormer (ASV Bodenwöhr) (p. 62), Thomas Gretler (pp. 16 t, 20 b, 22 b, 24 b, 25 b, 27 t, 30 t, 33, 34 t+b, 35, 36 b, 37, 40, 42, 44, 50 t, 73, 80 b), Jan Gutjahr (pp. 5 t, 7, 13 b, 15, 20 t, 21, 25 t, 26 t, 27 b, 28, 46, 48, 49 t, 54 b, 57, 59, 64 b, 65, 67, 68, 69 b, 71, 78 b, 81), Andreas Janitzki (pp. 10, 30 b, 50 b, 53 b, 64 t, 82 b, 83), Thorsten Löw (pp. 16 b, 18 b, 24 t, 41, 79, 84 t), Jörg Schneider (p. 91 c), Wolfgang Schulte (pp. 86, 87, 88, 89, 90, 92), Silke Sigloch (pp. 4, 5 b, 6, 8, 9, 11, 12, 13 t, 14, 17, 18 t, 19, 22 t, 23, 29, 31, 32, 36 t, 39, 43 t+c, 45, 47, 51, 52, 53 t, 55, 56, 58, 60, 61, 63, 66, 69 t, 70, 74 c, 78 t, 80 t, 82 t, 84 b l+t r, 85); drawings by Kay Elzner.

Disclaimer

All possible care has been taken in the making of this book. Nonetheless, no liability can be assumed for the information contained in it. Neither the author nor the translator nor the publisher can be held responsible for damages resulting from information in this book that is not in accordance with the current legal regulations in the Netherlands or Belgium, or for damages that result from the practical information in the book. Fishing without a license is not permitted. You can inform yourself thoroughly by consulting fishing organizations, official offices, and/or the Internet.

www.apollo-intermedia.de

Complete production: VEMAG Verlags- und Medien Aktiengesellschaft, Cologne

Printed in Germany
ISBN 3-625-10352-4

Table of Contents

Why We Fish!

It's Friday afternoon and I'm driving home with another stressful work week behind me. Only 15 more kilometres to go before I can repack the car and head for the water.

I'm still overwrought as I pack. Although work is done, the rods are not yet in the water so I'm eager to get back behind the wheel and leave. Later, parking close to the lake, I load up my cart and fairly trot to my fishing spot. I'm still strung up.

I assemble the rods, bait the hooks, cast, set the rods on their stands, put up my shade and seat, and flop down. Now—finally—I've arrived, and the last thing I need is an immediate bite because, let me tell you, in these first ten minutes I want nothing more than to relax and unwind.

I bet you have often heard the saying, "fishing is more than catching fish". This is absolutely true. Of course, a successful day of fishing is crowned by a good catch, but even a day with nothing to show for it is not a bad one. On the contrary, a day by the water without a catch is a whole lot more satisfying than one lost on the couch by the TV, or even an extra day at work, or hours spent in the fuggy air of the pub...

For me, fishing is at its relaxing best when I can be at the water for several days at a time. When I have my bivvy pitched and the rods set, I am

Early risers are sometimes rewarded with the bite of a great fish, and sometimes with a beautiful sunrise.

Anglers see more than many other people, for example this "kid coach."

an entirely new human being. I can gaze contentedly at the surface of a lake for hours at a time, mesmerised by the ripplets. The shapes of the clouds are as absorbing as the varied colours of the fields along the shore. Then, too, there is the fascination of the animal kingdom. There are so many animals to be seen near water—and here I'm not talking just about fish, but about scores of birds, about snakes, water rats, snails, worms and bats... How many people have seen a king fisher within two metres? As a fisherman, you have a good chance of doing that! And how many people have been fortunate enough to watch beavers building their dams, or a heron hunting its prey?

As dusk approaches, the anticipation mounts. This is it—the best time for a catch. Are there bubbles rising over there, right by my bait, made by feeding fish? At last, just as I am about to give up hope for a sunset bite tonight, the bite indicator suddenly starts to sing its song.

With every new bite I'm as excited as I was the first time I went fishing. Playing the fish is every bit as nerve wracking as it was then. And every new landing of the catch is as exhilarating as the first.

Oh yes, this is the crowning moment of a fishing trip—but the other aspects are very important, too: the heightened awareness of nature, the teeming wildlife in and around the water, the clarity of the slightest sounds, and the welcome relaxation after a hectic week.

People who enjoy fishing as their hobby are lucky—but this activity requires our protection. As fishermen and women, it is our job to look after the environment—if only by keeping our beats clean. And

Caring for bodies of water is part of a fisherman's work. Not every angler has access to such well-tended fishing spots.

Catching a big fish is the highlight of a day spent fishing.

believe me, it can be a lot of work collecting the litter left by passers by. Doing our part to maintain the diversity of the fish population is another aspect of being a responsible angler, and it is important to inculcate beginners—especially young beginners—with these attitudes.

Children who fish are far likelier to stay out of trouble. Just like the rest of us, they are too busy with one of the most interesting and varied pursuits there is.

We who fish know what it is like to wait in hope that the carp will bite. We can spin for a pike along an entire lakeshore, or hunt for walleyes from a boat, and we take part in the work of a fishing association when it repopulates a body of water. At home, we can make our own rigs, or learn how to tie various kinds of flies. All of these things are part of the pursuit of fishing.

I wrote this book so that you, too, may crown the greatest possible number of fishing expeditions with a satisfying catch. I hope it inspires and helps you, and I wish you every success.

Basic Equipment for the Beginner

Every fisherwoman or fisherman needs some basic equipment in order to pursue the craft. The exact equipment you choose will depend on several circumstances, such as the kind of water you plan to fish and the size of the expected catch. Yet as a beginner you should try to keep your expenses within manageable limits. How do you accomplish that?

If you ask an experienced angler—who may even have specialised in carp, pike or fly-fishing over time—whether there is an all-round set of equipment, you are likely to get an emphatic "no!" in response. But not to worry, you don't really need separate rods for carp, pike or trout. The specialists also started with the basics, and probably, like me, began with a single rod for any kind of fish.

So, what do you have to have for fishing? Most fundamentally, you need a rod, a reel, a line and your preferred kind of rig. The rig can consist either of a bobber and split shot, or simply of a sinker that (as the name suggests) drags the rig to the bottom of the water. In both cases, you will obviously also need hooks and some bait.

When casting the line, the bail arm must be open.

But what exactly does the correct equipment for a beginner look like?

Catching a catfish in the Ebro River in Spain puts a lot of strain on the rod.

Fishing Rods: An Extension of the Angler's Arm

Fishing rod technology has changed very rapidly. Until surprisingly recently almost everyone still used the typical bamboo cane. It was quite a revolution when glass and fibreglass rods came onto the market. But the majority of today's rods are nearly pure graphite, often toughened with Kevlar and teamed with silicone carbide guides.

What different kinds of rod are there? Roughly speaking, they can be divided into four categories: leger rods, spinning rods, boat rod, and fly rods. As a beginner, however, you are probably better off not to select a fly rod or a boat rod. What you need at the outset is a rod that works for ground fishing as well as for fishing with a bobber, and that even allows you to do some spin fishing.

And what kind of rod might that be? In order to decide what will work for you, you need to understand the basic characteristics of fishing rods, which I'll explain now.

A large number of different rods for the most diverse needs are available. Here is a selection of telescopic rods.

The "action" of a rod does not indicate how the rod reacts to the bite of a fish. Rather, it describes how the rod bends when under strain. There are three kinds of action: tip-action, middle-to-tip-action and through-action.

Tip-action means that when playing a fish, only the tip (the top part of the rod) bends and shows action. The rest of the rod remains stiff. This kind of rod is mainly used for float fishing for smaller whiting fish such as roaches or chubs.

Particularly fine tips double as bite indicators. To use them in that way, you can fish with a light ground rig, since the bite will be signalled by a light jiggling of the tip.

Middle-to-tip-action means, as the name indicates, that the rod bends from around the middle upwards when under strain. This is an advantage when catching larger fish because the tip will not break off and the hook will not slip out of the fish's mouth.

Finally, through-action rods bend all the way from the handle up to the tip when in action. These rods can be used for playing very large fish including sheatfish, carp and pike. Apart from that, they are very useful for casting your rig long distances, especially when you are using relatively large bait. However, buying such a rod does not guarantee that you will be able to cast a long way. More than anything else, the ability to make a long, smooth cast requires practice.

I therefore recommend a middle-to-tip-action rod as a good starting point for a beginner. Because of their light weight, they are well suited for casting, yet they still offer quite a lot of security when playing the fish. Fish weighing up to ten pounds are no problem for such rods—but first you have to catch one this large!

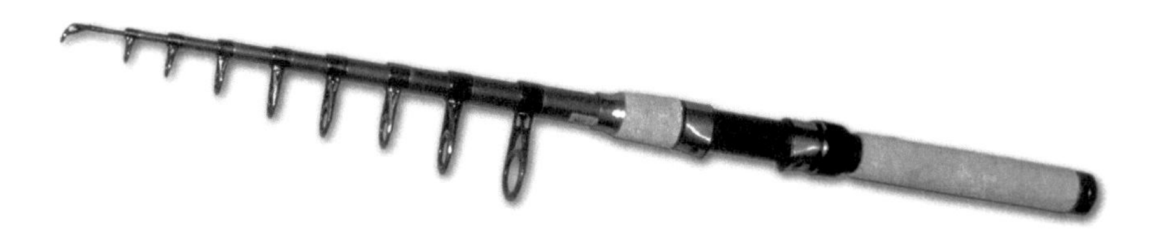

A telescopic rod is extremely convenient for transportation and fits into any bag.

The "casting weight" indicates how much the rig should ideally weigh if it is to cast well. The casting weight of a rod is a benchmark that is determined by the manufacturer. In this case, the weight refers to the combined weight of both the sinker and the bait.

For example, if you are using a 20-gramme sinker and a maize corn as bait, then your casting weight is approximately 20 grammes. If you fish with a 20-gramme sinker and a dead baitfish, however, you should weigh the baitfish to make sure that you don't over strain your rod. If you exceed the casting weight by too much, you run the risk of breaking your rod. On the other hand, if your rig falls short of the casting weight, this only affects the range of your casting. So always make sure that you don't cast rigs that are too heavy for the rod you are using.

In order to get your fish to shore safely, your rod has to make full use of its action when you play the fish.

Having said that, though, remember that the casting weight is only a benchmark, not an absolute value. There is no need to worry if your rod has a casting weight of 80 grammes and your rig actually weighs 100 grammes; however, you might want to reconsider your choice of rod if your rig weighs 200 grammes!

By the way, you will find the casting weight of each rod written somewhere near the handle. For those new to the sport of fishing I recommend casting weights between 20 and 80 grams.

Most rods are equipped with guides, also called rings. I will ignore those without guides, because these are extremely long poles (of eight metres and more) used only by specialists. Since my purpose here is to list material useful for beginners, I will only describe rods that have got guides.

For playing the fish, a rod with parabolic action is advantageous.

Guides can be directly attached to the rod, or they can have one or two quite long feet. The best choice depends on how you want to fish. If you plan to fish exclusively with a float, for example, you should use guides with two long feet because their length prevents the wet line sticking to the rod, while two-legged guides are a lot sturdier than the single kind. That means a beginner really should buy a rod equipped with two-legged guides. Since the first rod should be an all-purpose one, the other characteristics are less important. But the rod should have no less than five guides, and they must be thoroughly wrapped and lacquered.

A typical beginner's rod should be 3.00 to 3.30 metres long (although, naturally, there are also rods that are a lot shorter—boat fishing rods, for example). As soon as you think about getting a rod as long as this to the water one thing becomes clear: the length has to be reduced somehow in order to transport it. This is why all fishing rods are segmented: there are two-piece and three-piece rods (some have even more sections) and telescopic rods consisting of at least four segments.

The two-piece rod consists of two pieces that can be fitted together and afterwards taken apart again. The parts of a telescopic rod slide inside each other. This highlights a major difference between the two-piece and the telescopic rod: a telescopic rod can be reduced to a very small size because it consists of a larger number of shorter segments. This makes it much more convenient to transport. But the two-piece rod also has its advantages. Like the three-piece rod, it has fewer segments than the telescopic rod, which results in a much better action—which is a big advantage when you are playing a big fish.

Ultimately, the decision is to some extent also a question of taste and each individual will have to decide what is more important to him or her. If it is more important for you to be able to transport the rod conveniently, then you will likely be happier with a telescopic rod. If you prefer a rod with better action, on the other hand, you should start with a two-piece rod.

These days, I personally use only two-piece rods for fishing—but I do have a large car. Still, I can promise you one thing: you can catch fish with either type of rod!

General-purpose rods

Your first fishing rod should have middle-to-tip-action, and a casting weight of 20 to 80 grammes is ideal for beginners. Your rod should have at least five guides, preferably the kind that have two long legs. Whether you prefer a telescopic or a two- or three-piece fishing rod is a matter of personal preference.

The Reel—Fixed Spool

I must admit, there are so many different kinds of fishing reels available that it would be easy to become daunted. Fixed, multi-purpose, fly and closed-face reels are just a few of the wide variety that anglers can choose from. But in reality the selection isn't so difficult when you first take up the hobby of fishing, for the only one that really comes into question for the beginner is the fixed reel. This is the single most commonly used type because it works for any kind of angling except fly-fishing. It is also the most comfortable one to handle.

There are certain features your reel should have. Firstly, it must run smoothly, meaning that the spool should turn easily and evenly when you wind the handle. If the spool seems to wobble or wiggle when you try it there is only one thing to do—leave that reel in the store and keep looking. A smooth performance results from the interaction between the casing, gear, rotor and spool. It isn't essential to understand precisely how these parts work together and how the whole mechanism functions. Just be sure that the running is smooth and that, if at all possible, a spare spool is included in the price. If you have a spare spool, you'll be able to switch between lines of different strengths much more easily. But we'll deal with this topic further on.

The second feature to consider is the roller. It is located on the bail and is responsible for feeding the line on and off the spool. Rollers can be fixed or mobile, and

Two fixed-spool reels: a small bait-casting reel (top) and a small fixed-spool spinning reel (bottom).

View of the interior of a fixed reel.

they can also be mounted on a ball-bearing—but the important thing for the beginner is to make sure that the surface of the roller is very smooth. Otherwise, it will cause unnecessary wear on the line.

Perhaps the most important part of a good fishing reel is the drag control, which may be located to the front or the rear. The front drag control is set above the spool, and the second type is at the back of the reel.

It doesn't matter which kind you use—you may wish to experiment to figure out which suits you best. What does matter is that the controls work smoothly and don't jerk when they are set or released. (Imagine how the hook will wiggle in the mouth of the fish if the control keeps jerking!). It is quite easy to test the control system in the store: just wind the spool in the opposite direction to the drag control.

Finally, you will want to think about the quantity or length of line your reel can hold. This value is called the "capacity" and is stamped on the spool. I suggest that to start out you look for spools designed to hold 100 metres of 0.40-millimetre line. A reel like this will certainly have more than enough capacity for thinner lines, so they will be able to take a sufficient length 0.35-millimetre line for fishing pike or carp.

A multi-purpose reel: such reels are used in off-shore fishing for heavy fish.

Reel with bait-runner lever: the lever that completely releases the spool is at the end of the reel.

The perfect reel

Your first reel should definitely be a fixed reel. Before making a purchase, test it for smooth running. If possible, buy a reel that comes with a reserve spool. Make sure the roller has a smooth surface which won't wear on your line. The drag control should work without jerking the line. A beginner's reel should hold approximately 100 metres of 0.40-millimetre line.

I suggested above that you try to buy a reel with a spare spool. If you were able to do so, now you can use one spool for 0.35-millimetre line (for the larger fish), and the other for 0.25-millimetre (for roach and trout).

Spare spool: if you have a reserve spool, you can take two different kinds of line with you when you go fishing.

The Line

This brings us to the topic of the line. The fishing line is the only connection between the angler and the fish. Sometimes it has to withstand quite severe strain so it is always wise to make sure the line is sound. Check this frequently by letting the first few metres of your line—or any other segment of it—run between your thumb and fingers; if it feels rough, it is time to change the line. If there are little knots in the line—change your line! If your hook just got stuck and you pulled it out with a great branch in tow—change it!

Multifilament and monofilament lines: left a braided line, right a mono.

It is vital to replace your line regularly. This is more than a sensible precaution for you, it is also fairer to the fish—no angler wants to be responsible for quantities of fish swimming around with metres of line trailing from their mouths. How often you change the line depends to some extent on how often you go fishing, of course. But I recommend you change the line at least once a year as a rule, because the line continues to age even when it is not used at all.

Lines come in many different materials, but they basically fall into two categories: there are monofilament nylons (or monos), and multifilament (or braided) lines. As their names suggest, monofilament lines consist of a single nylon thread, while multifilament or braided lines consist of several strands. These strands are made of materials such as Dyneema or Dacron, and the individual strands are braided into a single line. The manufacturers take great care that the line is as round as possible.

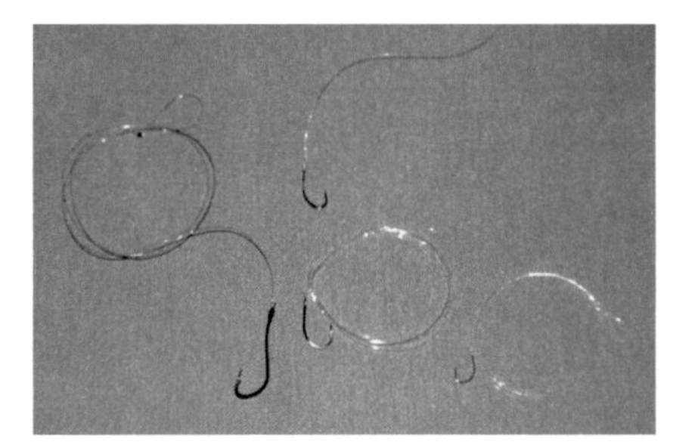

ready-made rigs with lines and hooks of different sizes.

Monofilament nylon is the traditional angling line—and it is often the better choice. Braided line has not been on the market very long. Its big advantage is that in spite of being very thin it can carry a lot of weight. This strength is marked on the packaging and it indicates the maximum weight the line can handle without breaking. But you should never put blind trust in the line strength for one good reason: the measurements are demonstrably imprecise, and the strength of two lines of the same diameter can vary considerably. Another characteristic of the braided line is its lack of flexibility. This may be a problem when you play the fish since the line's flexibility is an extra shock absorber that enhances your playing of the fish. I'll explain when to use which line in the chapters dealing with various angling techniques. I will also talk more precisely about the different diameters later on. But, for now, it is sufficient to

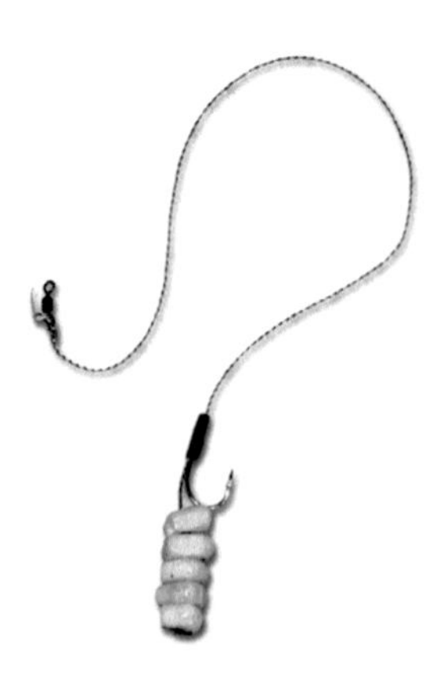

Self-tied hair rig baited with maize.

A barbell shortly before being landed—now the line has to hold.

state the fairly common-sense rule of thumb that you use thinner lines for small fish and thicker lines for larger ones.

The line itself consists of two parts: the main line and the leader. Obviously, the main line is by far the longer of the two. The leader is always somewhat thinner than the main line. I recommend that you choose a leader 0.05 millimetres thinner than your main line. Why is that? And, anyway, why not attach the hook to the main line? Well, the leader is the predetermined breaking point. Thus, if your line does have to break, it will be here and nowhere else. That makes sense for two reasons: firstly, if your line breaks because it gets stuck somewhere, then all you lose is the leader with the hook—you don't lose your entire line with sinker or metal shot and possibly a floater. Secondly, if the line breaks while you play the fish, then not only do you benefit from not having lost the entire rig, but the fish is left with only the hook and a few centimetres of leader in its mouth, rather than the heavy sinker or in the worst case, even ten or twenty metres of fishing line. Finally, the thinner line also means that you can present the bait to the fish less conspicuously, which means they will be quicker to trust the bait.

You can tie your own leaders or you can buy them ready-made. Special leaders are available for every kind of target fish, already set up with the correct line strength and hook size. Of course, there are some advantages in tying your own leaders. You have a lot if choices when making your own—you can vary them in length, strength, and also the size of the hook. But, in my opinion, a ready-made leader is perfectly adequate to begin with.

What to look for when choosing the line

No matter how strong your line is, make sure that it is not damaged anywhere. Your spool should certainly take 100 metres of the line of your choice. Leaders must be 0.05 millimetres thinner than the main line.

The Hook

Obviously, the thinner section of the line, called the leader, has two ends. One is tied to the main line and the hook is attached to the other. It is probably equally obvious that the hook is among your most important pieces of equipment, and there is a lot to take into consideration when deciding which is the right one. But there's no need to worry. Ultimately you will have only a few to choose from.

At the top of the hook is an "eye" or "spade", followed by the shank, the bend and, finally, the point, which is often barbed. The hook is an "eyed" or "eye-end" one if the top looks like the eye of a needle, or a loop. It is a "spade-end" hook if the top looks like a piece of flattened wire. You will find that most ready-made leaders come with spade-end hooks, since these can be tied more easily by

To catch a grass carp as enormous as this one, every piece of your tackle has to be in top condition.

There is an incredible range of different fishing hooks, but they can be divided into two basic types: those with eyes and those with spades. These differ in how the leader is tied to them—but first let me explain how a fishing hook is built.

machines. But you can tie either kind of hook perfectly well yourself. See the diagramme at the top of the page opposite for the method. In my opinion, whether you prefer to fish with an eyed or spade-end hook is purely a matter of taste. I feel that a beginner

Hooks must always be sharp, so always remember to take a whetstone.

will find it easier to tie on an eyed hook than a spade-end hook—but then I'm still using eye-end hooks today!

Just like the fish we catch, hooks come in the most varied sizes. To make it easier for the angler to purchase hooks, there are size norms. Just keep in mind that the smaller the number, the larger the hook. Thus a size 6 hook is quite a bit larger than a size 14 hook. But the scale doesn't stop at size 1: there are also the oversizes 0, followed by 1/0, 2/0, and so on.

A safe bet for the first-time fisherman would be a ready-made leader and a number 6 or 8 hook. This size hook can be baited with maize, dough or smallish worms. And that means you are well-enough equipped to catch a small roach or a carp.

Of course, such a blanket recommendation only applies as long as you're content to catch whatever happens to come along. Otherwise, the rule of thumb is the larger the desired catch, the larger the hook you need—but I'll detail this further in the course of the following chapters.

Another way that fish hooks can be classified is by the number of their points: thus there are single, double, and treble hooks. You can't miss the meaning here: the single hook has one point, the double hook two points and the treble hook three.

Generally speaking, any fish can be caught with a single hook. But there is more to be said about it than that, and the use of a double or triple

Treble hooks are hooks with three points.

hook depends not only on the fish, but equally on the bait. To keep the explanation simple at this stage, let's just say that double and treble hooks are only used for predatory fish. I'll explain later exactly when you need these hooks and how to use them.

One last comment with regard to the hook is necessary. It cannot be overemphasised how important it is to make sure that your hooks are always sharp. Only a sharp point will hook securely into the fish's mouth. Again, this meticulousness with the tackle is not only important for you, but also for the fish. Rusty or blunt hooks not only slip out of the fish's mouth, they can also cause serious wounds that are entirely unnecessary.

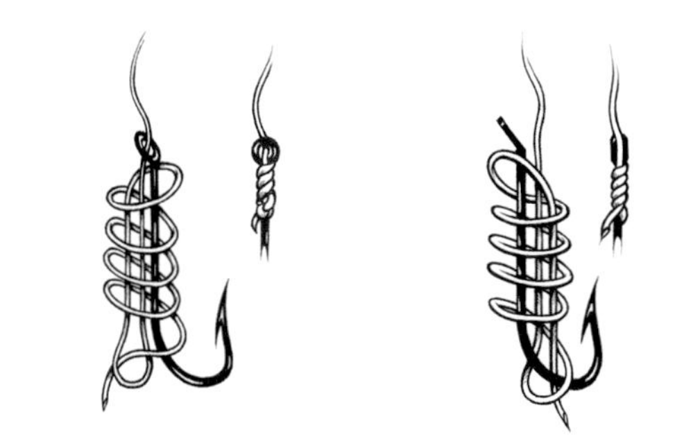

Attaching hook and line with a snell knot: left an eyed hook, right a spade-end hook.

There are many ways to check the sharpness of your hook. One is to test it on your thumbnail. Pull the hook across your thumbnail and if the hook is sharp enough it will catch onto the nail. If it simply slips across the nail the hook needs whetting. Another possibility is to use your thumb instead of the nail. Personally, I prefer the second method, but ought to warn you to be very cautious since the hook and barb can easily get stuck in the flesh of your thumb.

Once you have discovered that the hook needs sharpening, you can use either a whetstone or a piece of sandpaper to restore the point of the hook. I like to use a small whetstone (or hone). Dip the whetstone in water before pulling the point of your hook across the stone's surface. Do this three or four times, and your point will be sharp again.

The right hook

Beginners should start with eyed hooks or prefabricated leaders. Hooks sized 6 to 8 are convenient for a variety of fishing situations. The hooks must always be sharp, so make sure you have a way to sharpen them while you're near the water.

The Swivel

You know now what the end of the leader looks like. So let us proceed to the place where the leader connects to the main line. This connection is achieved with the help of a swivel.

What is a swivel? A swivel is a metal piece consisting of two interconnected eyes that can be moved in any direction independently from one another. The main line is attached to one of the eyes and the leader to the other. Since they rotate freely, the swivel prevents the line from twisting.

Snap swivels of different sizes and kinds.

Swivels come either with or without snaps. Swivels with snaps can be used much more conveniently and are therefore the obvious choice for beginners. If you angle with ready-made leaders, you can exchange them quickly and easily with a snap swivel. Personally, I only use swivels without snaps when I want to cast the line extremely far. This eliminates the possibility of the leader becoming entangled in the snap. But as a beginner you probably don't need to cast 80 to 100 metres—not yet. Swivels, by the way, are categorised by size, like hooks.

For beginners, snap swivels are advisable, because they are easier to use.

Other Accessories

After you have been fishing for a few years, you will have noticed that there is little you can't use at the edge of the water. The only question is how to transport all of it to your fishing spot. There are the most amazing devices: water thermometers, coolers, sonic depth finders, a camera—ideally with tripod—and so forth. So here is an important piece of advice: take as little material with you as possible. But do consider well so that you don't forget something really important. Here is a list of the essentials:

At the top of the list is the bite indicator—because somehow you have to recognise whether a fish has taken the hook. There are several kinds of bite indicators on the market, including floats, swingtips and quivertips, bells and monkey climbers. And of course there are electronic alarms. Since this piece of equipment must be chosen in relation to your favoured technique, we will go into more detail about bite indicators in the chapter on fishing techniques.

The landing net is one of the most important pieces of tackle for any angler. Even the best equipment will be useless to you if you have the wrong net—or no net at all. The net is used for landing the catch: slip the net under water and use the rod to guide the fish over the opening. Then lift the net so that the fish is safely trapped in the mesh.

In my experience, the most important aspect of a landing net is its size. Some nets are so small that I wonder why they were made in the first place. Ignore people who tell you they "just want to catch a couple of roaches". If a ten-pound carp gets hooked with your roach bait, it is already too late—and then it is your fault if this beautiful fish has to continue living with a hook in its mouth and a trailing line. So, avoid false economies and be sure to buy a net that is large and sturdy enough to use in a variety of situations. A beginner's landing net is large enough if its sides are at least 60 centimetres long.

A tape measure, a hanging balance, a pair of forceps, a priest, and a knife—these are the essential items that absolutely must be in your pockets, not because they enable you to tell the size of your fish, but because they ensure that you can treat your catch in a humane way.

A tape measure, hanging balance, and a sturdy landing net form part of every angler's standard equipment.

Most fish are protected by size limits. What does this mean? It means these limits are intended to give every fish a chance to live long enough to procreate at least once in

A peaceful atmosphere on the shore of a river—when will the first fish bite?

Small necessities

Measuring every fish is a must if you are to respect the size limits, so always keep a tape measure with you. If the fish is big enough, dispatch it immediately in a humane manner—you should always carry a priest and a knife in your pocket for this purpose. A landing net and forceps for removing the hook must also be a permanent part of your tackle.

its lifetime. Each breed of fish has therefore been assigned a minimum size, and may only be taken out of the water permanently when it reaches that minimum size.

Of course, you will occasionally catch a fish that is too small. Before you do anything else, you will have to establish your catch's actual size—that's what the tape measure is for. If you find that the fish is too small, you are required to release it back into the water as gently as possible. It will be necessary to unhook the fish very carefully, and that is most efficiently done with forceps. There are also several special scissor-like tools designed to remove hooks, and these may look quite different from each other. Some look like a combination of pliers and haemostat, others look like a staff with a guide in which you lay the line. Whichever tool you use, it is essential to treat the fish as gently as possible; after all, it is a living creature.

If the fish is big enough and you wish to take it home, you must kill it immediately.

A pair of forceps is the best tool for removing a hook.

For that you need something called a "priest" that does not, in fact, kill the fish but only stuns it. The priest is a bar with a heavy end that is used to whack the fish on the head. After that, use the knife—that you should always carry in your pocket—to pierce it.

Finally, you will need a hanging balance. Near many waters, you are required to enter the weight of the fish into a catch list. Clearly, this is a sensible routine since it determines whether the fish are well enough fed for their size. Monitoring this information regularly gives fishing clubs the opportunity to respond quickly if they find evidence that the water quality is deteriorating.

Non-Predatory Fish—Food and Bait

Of course, I could simply tell you which bait to use for carp and which for pike. However, in my opinion, you need to understand why certain baits should be used if you are to become a really good angler. So I plan to talk first about the fishes' feeding habits and then consider which bait to use.

Obviously, there are many factors to keep in mind. The size of a fish, for example, is as relevant as the season of the year. Yet it is possible to make a few basic statements about the feeding habits of the intended catch that will be very helpful when selecting your bait.

Many native fish species feed on small creatures, or at least include small creatures in their diet. Thus their food

The barbel lives on the bottom of the water, which is where it is most often caught.

The carp has a protruding mouth and feeds almost exclusively on small organisms.

consists mainly of small organisms including leeches, crabs, worms, insect larvae, snails and even mussles, in other words, bottom-dwelling invertebrates.

Cyprinidae (including carp, bream, and tench) are typical of this kind of feeder. They are immediately recognisable by the shape of their body, which reflects their diet. They all have a mouth that extends when they feed somewhat like a tube. This "tube" probes the waterbed, sucking up masses of small particles, a little bit like a vacuum cleaner. The edible and inedible parts are separated inside the mouth, and the fish spits out the unwanted material.

Different bodies of water, however, can be home to a different variety of small organisms. For example, we can

The bream also has a protruding mouth and it, too, feeds on small organisms.

The feeding pattern of non-predatory fish

As indicated by their physique, non-predatory fish feed mainly on small organisms, plants, and plankton. While I certainly would not suggest you try to fish with monads or algae, you should pay attention to fish feeding patterns. Almost any non-predatory fish can be caught with worms, snails, or even tubifex. If you'd like a challenge, bait your hook with the leaves of cattail for a change; more than one silver carp has been caught that way!

find insect larvae of all kinds in clear, cool brooks inhabited by trout. In lakes, the predominant insect larvae are those of the midge fly, but there are also plenty of sludge worms (also known as tubifex) and snails. Tubifex is a main component of carps' diet, especially while they are still young.

During the warmer season, when there is a plethora of insects, many fish that live on tiny organisms can be caught near the surface of the water. This is because so many insects accidentally fall onto the water's surface and get stuck there. These fish include not only trout, as many people might guess, but also chub, dace, rudd and even carp.

Other fish feed on plants and periphyton. I certainly don't need to explain what plants are, but periphyton is a different matter. The biological term "periphyton" describes a coating consisting of monads, bacteria and extremely small algae which covers stones and other hard surfaces in a body of water. Many fish use periphyton as a rich food source. The most typical and characteristic species is the nase. The mouth of this fish has lips that are completely covered with a horny sheath which is used to scrape the periphyton off the stones.

Many fish, for example roach, also eat water plants. Although there are no native European fish species that feed exclusively on plants, silver carps, which are originally from

This angler obviously knew that carp is typically caught on the bottom.

Asia, have become quite frequent in our lakes, rivers and streams, and these do feed exclusively on plants. The stocking—indicating the introduction of fish into a body of water—of silver carps and other Asian fish species that feed exclusively on plants is widely forbidden today. This is because they are thought to have caused the reduction or disappearance of expanses of cattail and water lilies.

The nase feeds on periphyton. Its lips are covered with a horny sheath and are used to scrape the periphyton from stones.

If the normal food supply becomes scarce, almost all fish will eat plankton as a substitute. Plankton (also originally a biological term) refers to micro-organisms such as monads, water fleas and copepods which float freely in the water. But there are also fish for whom plankton is the primary food. Among these are whitefish, chars, bleaks and alice shads. More than any other food source, plankton is highly dependant on favourable water conditions. Fortunately, fish species that eat plankton can switch to other food sources relatively easily when necessary, such as small organisms and periphyton.

Roaches eat just about anything: worms at the bottom, insects on the surface and plankton in the water.

Predatory Fish—Food and Bait

First and foremost, predatory fish feed on other fish. However, this needs some qualification. Pike, for example, are not averse to frogs or water rats, while large catfish have been observed eating fully grown ducks. On the other hand a perch or an eel obviously can't manage a two-kilogramme bream. So there are indeed differences between the predatory fish, but their staple prey remains fish.

Catfish and pike are the largest predatory fish found in our waters. As mentioned above, they have even been known to occasionally catch a duck. Naturally, this does not mean that you should try your luck with some poor bird for bait, but—and this is important—the baitfish should not be too small, either. In addition, bear in mind that pike always eat their prey headfirst. This makes a crucial difference to the way you present the baited hook in the water. Also remember that pike and catfish resort to eating small organisms in times of scarce supply. For catfish in particular, night crawlers are a choice bait.

The feeding pattern of predatory fish

Predatory fish feed mainly on other fish, and a fish is unquestionably the best bait for catching them. However, because predatory fish often eat small organisms as well, they can also be baited with worms. It follows that earthworms or compost worms make perfectly good general bait for all kinds of fish. So when you bait your hook with a worm, you may well be in for a surprise!

Pickerel follow smaller fish until they can grab them from behind.

Pike attack their prey suddenly and then flip it around in order to swallow the fish headfirst. Pickerel and perch hunt with a quite different technique. The pickerel follows its prey until it can grab it from behind—so a pickerel typically eats its prey tail first. Perch use a very similar approach, except that they hunt in groups. This can often be observed when the

Graylings mostly feed on insects on the water's surface.

water surface starts to churn as a school of perch dives into a shoal of smaller fish.

Eels, on the other hand, are their own very special case: they have two distinctly different head shapes depending not on their species, but on the local feeding pattern. Eels with somewhat pointed heads feed exclusively on small organisms, while those with broader heads feed mainly on fish.

Perch hunt in groups. However, they tend to become loners when fully grown.

All three of these kinds of predatory fish share one thing in common, however: they prefer to eat rather small fish (this also becomes clear if you look at their fairly small mouths, at least in comparison to that of the pike). But pickerel, perch and eel will generally also respond to night crawlers as bait since they have to resort to small organisms as food time and again when prey is scarce.

The catfish is one of the largest freshwater fish. It lurks in dark crevices and typically hunts at night.

What You Can Tell from Observation

Every body of water has unique characteristics. In rivers these include the inner and outer shores of bends, groynes, bridges and sluices. In a lake they may be patches of cattail, islands, river estuaries and similar spots. Obviously, the fish choose places where they are comfortable. With some experience you will soon learn to recognise them. A few hints to help you choose a spot follow.

The shape of a fish's body is a good indicator of where it likes to roam, and fish can have the most diverse body shapes. There are the snake-like eel, the cylinder-shaped trout, the pike with its torpedo-like body, or fish with high backs and flat bodies such as carp and bream. A body like a cylinder, or better, a spindle, is the sign of a fast swimmer. Fish with this kind of body typically enjoy currents. This is true for all kinds of trout, zander and also chub.

The pike is something of an exception. Although it can often be found in a current, where one might expect it to be, it is also found in calm waters because it follows its prey. The shape of the pike is an especially good indicator of the way it hunts. No other fish can accelerate as fast as the pike; one could truly say it is the Ferrari among fish. This is necessary, too, since the pike hunts from its lurking point. It waits almost motionless between cattails or underneath fallen trees until it has chosen its quarry—and then bursts out like a bullet to snatch its prey.

This angler knew where to look for the silver crucian carp's habitat.

Bream are quite flat and have a very high back. This indicates that they can be found in parts with calm water.

Then there are the fish with high backs. This body shape indicates that they aren't found in areas with strong currents. These fish live in calm water, often among various water plants. Among those species are crucian carp, carp and bream.

Fish that dwell mostly on the bottom tend to have a snake-like shape. The best example is the eel, but burbot and catfish are also typical of this form. The barbel is an interesting case: it has a spindle-shaped body that is flattened on the belly. Barbel can indeed be found in river areas with appreciable currents, but they remain quite close to the bottom. Another indicator of this is the location of the mouth at the bottom of the head, which reminds us that this fish finds its food on the ground.

The zander is a hunter that often "stands" in the current, but hunts close to the shore in the course of the night.

Paying attention to fish body shapes

The shape of a fish's body and the position of its mouth give us clues as to where fish can be found most commonly. This enables the fisherman or fisherwoman to estimate approximately how deep they need to position their hook, for example. Knowing something about your quarry fish, what it looks like and how it behaves makes it easier to make a confident decision about whether to fish in a current or in calm water.

The shape of the mouth tells us a lot about the other fish, too. Three different mouth types are recognised by their position at the bottom, front and top of the head.

The mouth is said to be at the top of the head when the upper jaw is shorter than the lower one. The fish most typically associated with this feature is the pike, but the rudd also is a "top mouth" fish. The mouth at the top of the head indicates that the fish finds its nourishment upwards. That is, its quarry can be found on the water surface (as with the rudd) or the fish snaps from bottom to top (as with the pike).

The mouth is said to be at the front of the head when the jaws are equal in length, which is typical of perch, trout and roach. This mouth shape indicates that food is found in open water.

Finally, there are the fish whose mouth is set at the bottom of the head. Their upper jaw is longer than their lower jaw. These fish typically find their nourishment at the bottom of the lake or stream. In addition to the barbel mentioned above, the gudgeon (or river goby) also belongs to this group—but so do fish with protruding mouths such as carp, tench, or bream.

Fishing Spots on a Lake

Plants give an excellent indication of where you can find fish. Water plants offer fish protection, food and spawning places. In among the plants we can usually find a wide variety of non-predatory fish: carp, roach and tench search the bottom for food between the plants or find protection from the sunlight under the leaves of water lilies. Pike lurk for their quarry at the edges of most plant patches because they know very well that roach and bream like to forage among the weeds. Even dense fields of reeds still attract fish—here, we often encounter eels. But do take care: you can easily loose your tackle in those tangled stalks, so be sure to use a suitably strong line.

The drop-off, the transition from a shallow shore area to

Water plants

Wherever you can see plants with the naked eye, fishing is likely to be worthwhile. However, you will face the added challenge of getting the fish cleanly from between the plants. All too often, anglers end up losing their tackle amidst the tangled stalks.

View of cattail islands in a lake—certainly a good fishing spot.

It is hard to fish among patches of water lilies even though they are excellent habitats for fish.

the deeper waters of a lake—which is often very steep—is an ideal spot to put out your hook. In many cases the drop-off can be recognised by the sudden disappearance of water plants at a certain point. Predatory fish are always located right at the ledge. This is where they wait for their prey because the non-predatory fish roam above the drop-off searching for food and swim out into the open water as soon as they have had their fill. This is the moment that pike and other predators are waiting for.

Underwater hills and other objects in the water attract fish almost magically. A famous angler once said, "If you find a lake with a consistent depth and no other obstacles, toss in a refrigerator and all the fish in the lake will be crowded around it within an hour." Naturally, the fish don't know what we keep in our refrigerators, but this kind of barrier provides them with protection and food.

The same is true for underwater hills, which are sometimes also called "perch mountains." Especially in deep water areas, fish look for food on the slopes of underwater hills. And as mentioned above,

Fathoming

The sole function of a fathoming rod is to measure the depth of water. They can be assembled in different ways. One is to mark every metre on the line, which is dropped with a sinker from a boat. The other is to use fixed floaters and try them out several times; this can also be done from the shore. The fastest and easiest method is with a digital depth finder, but these are far from cheap.

Clumps of reeds are also good fishing spots, but hazardous for your equipment.

wherever there are smaller non-predatory fish, large predators can be found as well. But there is one obvious problem: these underwater mountains don't reach the surface (if they did they would be islands!), so it can be hard to find them. If you take the trouble to look for a hill with your depth finder, it will be well worth your while and you might find an angler's paradise.

Cattail along the shores are areas where lots of fish live.

From the perspective of a fish, islands are no different from underwater hills: they are merely underwater mountains whose peaks are above water. So what has been said about underwater hills also applies to islands. In addition, islands often also have a shallow shore region with a steep drop-off. Islands, therefore, have all the ingredients of a top fishing spot. If you are angling in a lake with islands, then an island will certainly be a great place to fish. Naturally, you must still decide how best to

Underwater hills are found most easily from a boat.

The shore area

Along the shore of a lake there are numerous areas which are well-suited for angling. Apart from that, many types of fish tend to come close to the shore at dusk and during the night to feed. For these reasons, fishing from the shore is very rewarding. Since it is not necessary to cast very far out, beginners are especially encouraged to start with shore fishing.

This area "smells" like fish.

fish the island area; fishing from a boat is not permitted everywhere. So I will leave it at this: if you have a chance to fish from or near an island, you should definitely do so.

Shore areas have a particularly wide range of features of interest to anglers. In addition to the usual zones of shallow water, there are steep-sided deep areas and possibly also overhangs. Fallen trees may be found there, or branches which extend far across the water. These sites are all perfect roaming areas for fish. However, the artificial, man-made areas are no less interesting. Among them, for example, are swimming areas. Try angling in the very early morning or late in the evening on a shore that is used for swimming during the day. Here, the water is typically muddy—in itself a good indicator for zander. But non-predators like carp and bream also know that the swimmers disturb the bottom and stir up edible particles. Harbours, ports, foot bridges, river mouths and water outlets are all places that are worth a try.

Obstacles in the water such as this fallen tree attract fish like magic.

Fishing Spots on a River

Rivers can often provide an extraordinary experience of nature.

Most anglers with many years of experience would probably agree that fishing a river is harder than a lake. This is almost certainly based on the anglers' preconceived ideas. In their opinion, a small lake is a closed environment from which the fish cannot escape. In contrast, a river is an effectively endless ribbon of flowing water. But if you let go of this image, you will find there are prominent spots along a river, too, that lend themselves to successful fishing. One should also bear in mind that rivers have changed markedly in character as a result of human influence. Sheet pile walls, dams, bridges and port facilities have been built and these are now part of the fish's habitat.

Modern rivers are typically well furnished with barrages and dams. Barrages—their ecological hazards or benefits raise a separate issue that I won't discuss here—obviously become rich food sources. If a barrage is also used as a floodgate for ships, this has the effect that the food particles are constantly stirred up, thus creating perfect conditions for small and larger non-predatory fish. And wherever there are small non-predatory fish, one can find larger predators as well.

On the other hand, bear in mind that angling is a lot more work where there are a lot of boats in the water: you will often have to haul in your rigs to protect them from boat propellers or snarling. But if

Scours often form at the point where several streams convege.

Barrages

Barrages are relatively hard to fish. But their retaining function results in large quantities of food for fish being collected. This always attracts the fish—predatory and non-predatory alike. So it is well worth trying your luck near a barrage.

you can put up with this kind of stress you may be rewarded with some very good catches.

Of course, riverbeds are not perfectly flat. There are deeper patches, almost like holes, which are called scours. These hollows often form underneath waterfalls, behind barrages or where smaller streams flow into larger rivers. Inevitably, edible particles accumulate in the scours in the riverbed. Furthermore, there is less current in these locations than elsewhere, so you can often find fish foraging here that tend to avoid strong currents. Among these are bream and tench.

If the scour is fairly large and is shaped like a trough or furrow, you have probably located a spot where big catfish like to live. This is a favoured point of departure for those freshwater giants' nightly hunting expeditions.

Rivers are always one component of an entire system. Smaller streams meet larger rivers and these in turn flow into even larger ones. The confluences, where small streams or rivers merge with larger ones, are also excellent fishing spots. Where the two currents meet, flat areas exist alongside deeper water. The deeper areas form trenches, which are especially large because this is where the force of two currents is combined. Beside and be-

Overhanging branches offer a shady spot for this trout.

Where a smaller river flows into a larger one there is a lot of oxygen and plenty of food for fish.

Confluences

Several conditions favourable to fish can be found at the confluence of two rivers. This means there are plenty of good spots for each angler, whether he or she prefers to fish for predators or non-predatory fish. Here, too, the deepest trenches tend to be frequented by large catfish.

tween the trenches are sandbanks, i.e. shallow areas with calm water. Trout, grayfish and even barbels can be found in locations with faster currents, while perch, pike, carp and tench prefer the calmer, shallower areas.

Bridges are also among the many parts of a river that have been shaped by human beings, and they often prove to be excellent fishing spots. Between the piers of a bridge the riverbed becomes narrower, causing the formation of current trenches and scours. Furthermore, the piers and the bridge itself provide a degree of shade. This means that we find an accumulation of favourable conditions for fish—and thus for anglers. Weak and strong currents interchange and food particles accumulate along the piers as well as in the scours. As a result, you can count on a large variety of fish taking advantage of the different sections of this habitat—exactly as in the other spots described above.

Bridges

Bridges can be among the best fishing spots on a river. So if a large highway overpass spoils a beautiful river landscape don't fret too much. The silver lining is that if you cast your bait here, you may be in for quite some surprises.

Fortunately, there are still places where the river follows an undisturbed natural course through the landscape. In these areas, the best fishing spots are primarily found at the bends. Bear in mind, though, that the outside and inside banks of the bend offer entirely different conditions for the fish.

The outside bank takes a much more forceful current than the inside bank. This means that there are often

Bridges are always worth your while.

The outside bank of a bend offers an ideal habitat for many fish.

undercuts in the outside bank, and these protected spaces are favoured hiding grounds for hunters like trout or pike.

The inside bank, on the other hand, often forms a very calm area, and fish that prefer calmer waters will therefore typically congregate there. If there are trees and bushes growing along the shores, these provide additional points of attraction for the fish since they offer both shade and a supply of insects and other small creatures that fall from them into the water.

Of course, turning theory into practice is not so easy when you're near the water, so let me continue with a couple of hints that are very simple to

River bends

River bends also offer wonderful fishing spots. However, one should be aware of the differing currents along the inside and outside banks. If trees and bushes grow along the shores of the bends, they add to the food supply in the water. These places are always worth a try.

Occasionally one can find unspoilt sections of a river.

This river is characterised by its natural meanders.

follow. If you angle along the bank, look out for little clouds of mud and bubbles. Non-predatory fish like tench, carp and bream feeding at the bottom stir up the mud with their mouths. In so doing, they create little clouds of mud and bubbles. Cast your line wherever you spot this visible clue. Bear in mind, though, that putrid slime also emits bubbles due to fermentation, and fish can almost never be found there. If you are not sure which kind of bubbles you are dealing with, it helps to cast a heavy sinker. This may briefly chase off any fish, but it saves you wasting time and effort in a spot where there are no fish at all. As soon as you haul in your sinker, you'll know by the smell if the bubbles were given off by putrid slime.

Another clue that you can pick up simply through observation is eruptions of bait fish. It is a fascinating sight, especially when you see it for the first time. Scores of tiny fish simultaneously burst out of the water at almost the same spot. This is nearly always caused by predatory fish hunting, and the trigger for this event could easily be a group of perch or a single zander. So if you happen to observe this phenomenon, cast your bait fish or your artificial bait into the area. You may often have astonishingly quick success with this method.

People should never forget how dangerous water can be.

Perfect Waters for a Beginner

Even brook trout are introduced into many private fishing ponds.

So, let's get to the water! There are a few things to bear in mind when choosing your first stretch of water: saltwater fishing is certainly great sport, but the sea is just as certainly not the best fishing ground for a beginner. The same is true of all kinds of running water: they are either very wide with strong currents or, at the opposite extreme, they are small streams with very few fish. Large lakes are far from ideal for beginners, too, since it can be quite difficult to locate the fish hidden below their surface.

No, the perfect water for a beginner often turns out to be a private trout pond. These small waters are preferable as well because most do not require a fishing license. They can be treated as safe practice grounds for the true angler of tomorrow. Sadly, many experienced anglers despise these trout ponds, a judgment I cannot share. After qualifying for my fishing license, I started angling in the Neckar River in southern Germany—and if it hadn't been for an acquaintance who took me along to a fishing pond, I might never have pursued this wonderful hobby at all. These days, I no longer visit trout ponds very often, but they can be the right place when you are learning this sport.

Private trout ponds offer several advantages. Firstly, they are restocked daily to match the depletion rate, so there are always plenty of fish. You are almost guaranteed a catch—and, when all is said and done, it's important to have some success when you start out. Furthermore, these waters typically offer a consistent, usually fairly shallow depth (I would generally recommend setting your rig for a depth of 1.50 metres). This unified environment ensures that the angler doesn't need to search for the fish because they can be found just about anywhere. Another advantage of these ponds is the fact that artificial bait is usually forbidden. I am not at all opposed to artificial bait, but for one thing, this regulation ensures that all who want to fish the pond experience very similar conditions; for another, I believe that fishing with natural bait and a float is the surest and best initiation to this pastime.

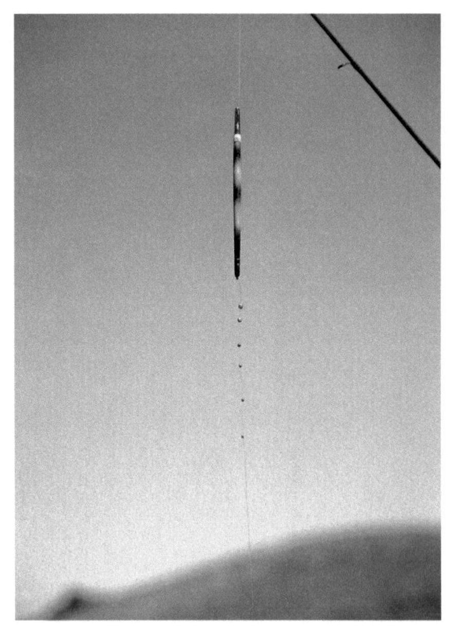

The stick or balsa float is my favourite when fishing a trout pond.

Natural bait for trout includes maggots, bee grubs, compost worms, and trout dough. This bait is attached to a ready-made rig with a number 8 to 12 size hook. A slim, firmly attached float, ideally a stick or balsa type, tops off the rig. Attach enough split shot to the rig so that only the coloured tip of the float stays above the water's surface and you're ready to go.

The simplest approach is to cast and wait. As mentioned above, you can't go wrong setting your rig for a depth of 1.50 metres. With this depth all beginners will make a catch and gain his or her first experience of hooking, playing and landing a fish.

Nonetheless, let me share a trick that will bring in more fish in the long run: the secret is moving bait. With a few techniques, natural bait can be

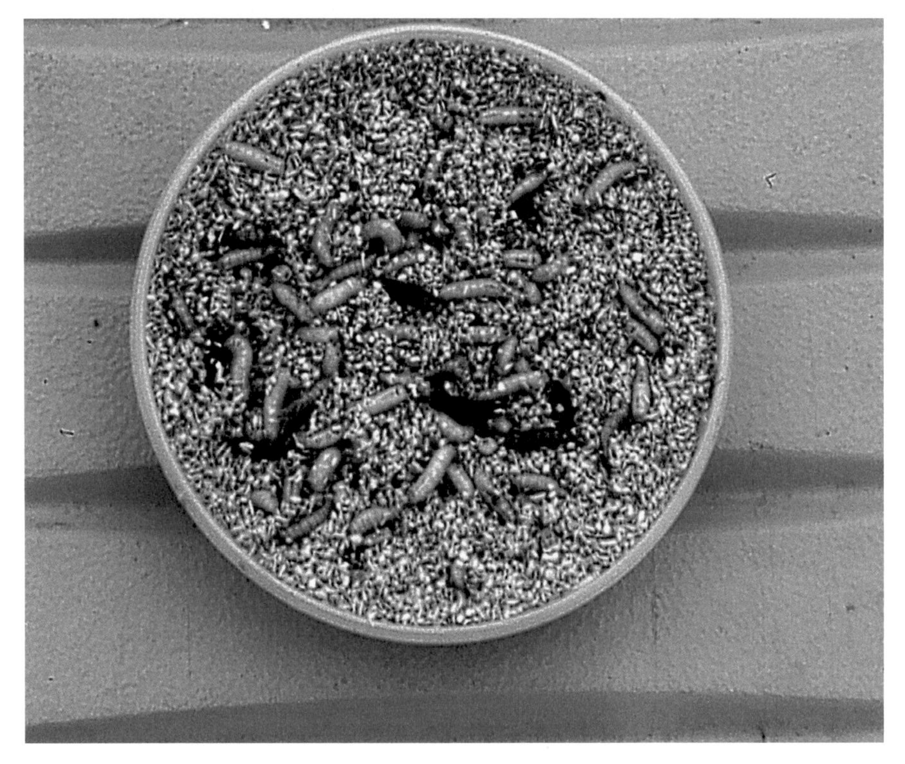

Grubs are a good and always acceptable bait for trout fishing.

The rainbow trout is the most common quarry with this kind of angling.

Trout ponds

In many places it is permissible to fish without a license in relatively small stretches of water. These include most private fishing ponds, and that makes them ideal for your first forays into the hobby. Even if you already have a fishing license, a trout pond is the perfect beginner's spot because it is so simple to fish there—and you will often be successful.

made as attractive for fish as artificial bait. This can be done most easily with trout dough, which is the universal bait in this kind of water, anyway.

For your first trip to a trout pond I would suggest using trout dough in three different colours at most—one dark, one light, and one with glitter will be quite sufficient. But back to the tricks: after attaching the dough to the hook, press it between your fingers, flatten it and give it a slight dent. Once you pull the line it starts to swivel around its axis. This lets you fish with the dough as if it were artificial bait. Cast your line and reel it in slowly. If you notice a twitch, stop immediately and watch the float. If the float starts to wander or even goes down, hook immediately.

This trick works in a very similar way with maggots. In this case you will have to attach two maggots to the hook in the shape of a capital L, and then this bait, too, will swivel or rotate.

Fishing with a Float

Even if you've obtained your fishing license mainly in order to fish large pike, you still need baitfish. Almost all baitfish are non-predatory fish. So if you want to catch predatory fish, you first have to catch non-predatory fish. In any case, whether you want to become an expert on pike, a carp aficionado, or a fly fisherman, remember that the true angler will always work up from the very beginning, starting with small roach and other whiting before going for your main quarry.

The float is certainly the oldest bite indicator in the world, and even today is among the best and most reliable. Of course, there are now highly developed electronic bite indicators, but for some kinds of fishing these are almost useless. For example, I don't know a single angler who would ever think of taking an electronic bite indicator when fishing for roach.

So, what kinds of float are there? Generally, floats can be separated into two categories: those that are firmly attached to the line, and slip-floats that slide along the line. I would suggest using a firmly attached (or "fixed") float whenever possible—although they can only be used when the water depth and the casting distance allow it.

Crucian carp are small non-predatory fish that put up quite a fight when they are hooked.

To make it clear why these floats can only be used up to a certain water depth, let me explain how fixed floats work. The name derives from the fact that the float is attached to the line at the desired point and then cast. This means that the water can be no deeper than the length of your rod, because otherwise the leader would drag on the ground when you cast. This would inadvertently lead to complications when you cast, such as hitting trees and the like. But for depths between two and three metres, fixed floats are definitely the best choice; I personally recommend using them for depths of up to three metres, though beyond two metres of depth the decision should be left to the individual and their level of comfort.

If you fish in waters that are deeper than three metres, you will need to use slip-floats running freely along the line. This means that you will have to fix a stopper on your line—which I will explain later—whose position depends on the depth of the water. This stopper can be reeled up to the spool without complications and just as easily cast. The float itself is designed so that it runs freely along the line: the line runs either through the bobber itself or through the eyes of the swivel. In both cases, it is possible to fish with a float quite unlimited by the water depth.

I would like to explain the use of the float depending on certain angling situations. Let's first look at the use of a fixed float when fishing for whiting. Imagine that you are at a

Slim floats are very sensitive bite indicators.

The bristle float may be the most common fixed float of all.

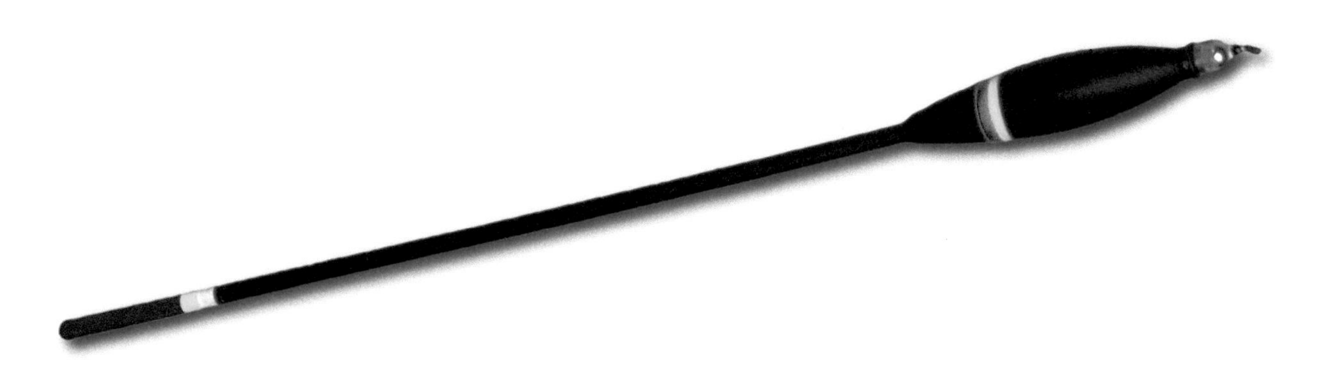

The polywag is a float that slips freely along the line, which makes long casts possible.

small, flat lake. You would like to fish for roach along its shore. In this case you would want to use your general-purpose rod with 0.25-millimetre line. As usual, the basic rule is "Always fish as lightly as possible and only with as heavy a line as necessary!" This also means that the bite indication through the float should be as sensitive as possible so that you can recognise even the lightest pull. On the other hand, an inconspicuous 0.16-millimetre line won't be of any use if an eight-pound carp takes the hook, rips the line and swims around with this souvenir hanging from its mouth. Therefore I suggest you use an 0.25-millimetre line and a bristle float that is as fine as possible. In this situation especially, you should use a slim, light float in the shape of an arrow.

Now it is time to mount the necessary rig: if you use a fixed float, slip it onto the main line first. It is usually adjusted with the help of a rubber band. Then use the clinch knot to tie on a snap swivel. The clinch knot is one of the few knots that is truly necessary for your hobby; I have included a detailed drawing of the knot here. Once the

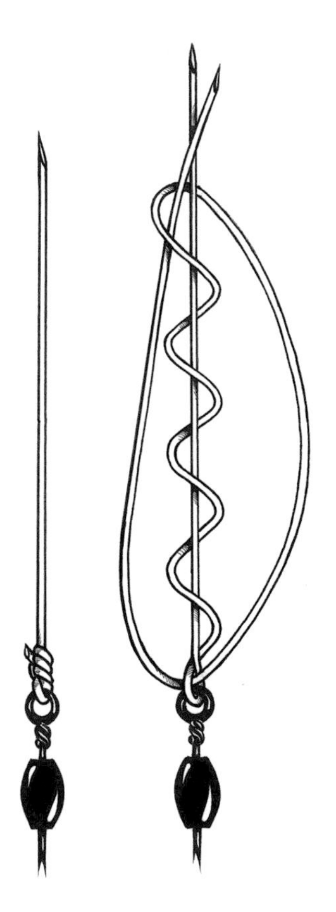

The clinch knot is probably the most frequently used knot among anglers.

If you fish with a float you will need split shot in different sizes.

float and the swivel are attached, the float must be weighted. In order to do that, attach as much split shot as you need in order to leave only the tip of the float above the water surface. By the way, I usually do this at home in my aquarium. If you don't have an aquarium you'll have to do it directly on the shore.

There are a few more things to keep in mind when you attach the split shot. For example, avoid using very few relatively large pieces of metal because the fish are more likely to notice their resistance. It is better to use a fair number of small split shot, preferably arranged in order of size. This means that the largest split shot comes next to the float and gets smaller as you work down. In this way, the fish feels only the smallest piece of metal as first resistance.

Then attach a ready-made leader with a size-8 hook or even smaller. Now fathom the depth of the water. You can do that best with a sinker, i.e. a heavy piece of lead. The sinker is attached to the hook and must be too heavy to be supported by the float. Generally, you will have a vague idea of how deep the water is. If you think the water might be about two metres deep, fix your float two metres above the sinker on the line. Then cast the rig.

Now, there are three possible results: most rarely the bobber will float exactly in the right position so that only the coloured tip shows above the surface. In that case, you have estimated the depth of the water absolutely correctly. Or your float may sink completely and disappear from sight. This

The fixed float

There is nothing better than a fixed float when angling for small non-predatory fish in the shallow water along the shore. This is because those floats are not only very inconspicuous but also extremely sensitive. Fixed floats respond to even the tiniest nibble by a fish.

means that the water is deeper than you had expected. If so, move your float up a little and cast the sinker again. Repeat this as often as necessary until the bobber floats on the surface exactly as far as it should. Of course, it can also happen that the bobber floats flat on the water when you cast. In this case the water is not as deep as you thought and you'll have to move the float down and try again. Repeat this until you have found the perfect position for the bobber. Once you have established the depth I suggest you move your float about five centimetres down the line. This lets you fish a few centimetres above the bottom where your bait is very conspicuous.

Remember that when you fish for whiting you will have to do some feeding. This means you should throw out a little food, called chum, at the spot where you intend to fish. Either use a little maize or a mix of maize and breadcrumbs. If you wish, you can also knead a few maggots into the mix. Don't make the chum too sloppy; it has to be firm enough to mould into globs the size of tennis balls. Throw these into the water—one or two at most. If you get the consistency right, it will crumble while sinking to the bottom and form a food carpet there. Your bait will float just above this carpet. According to the ingredients of the chum ball

When fishing for roach you may catch rather a lot of fish.

you should fish with maize, dough, or maggots to match. Other bait, however, may also promise success. After all, the food carpet is only supposed to entice the fish to feeding. Typically, fish will start to eat just about anything once they have begun to feed.

The next thing is to wait for the first bite. When you're fishing for whiting this doesn't usually take very long. Typically, the first roach or bream will go for the hook quite quickly. If you haven't got a bite after half an hour, it may help to change the height of your float. The fish may not be swimming right at the bottom, but a little higher in the open water. So move the float a little farther down and change your feeding by throwing maize or maggots into the water without any additions. This is the only way to present your bait at the right depth while at the same time allowing the light maize and maggots to sink slowly enough for the fish to have time to notice them.

Determining the correct depth is simply a matter of trial and error. And always bear in mind that on some days, there simply may not be a catch. It may be due to the weather, or the fish may simply be roaming a different part of the lake. But this is a promise: if the conditions are right and you do everything as described, then you will catch a fair amount of fish within a short time span.

To explain how the slip-float works, I'd like to describe another angling situation. You want to fish in a spot about twenty metres from the shore; the water there might be around four metres deep. Out there, both the length of the cast and the depth of the water make it necessary to angle with a slip-float. These floats can carry more weight than the fixed ones, but they also weigh more. The combined weight of the rig is higher, which means it can be cast farther. When using slip-floats, my favourite is the so-called polywag—partly because the weight of the float itself can be changed, and partly because it can be cast a long distance, thanks to its slim shape. As always, this is a question of individual taste. Naturally, you can use any other slip-float of your liking. However, as with the fixed float, do keep in mind that a bite indicator should be as sensitive as possible. Therefore keep floats that can carry particularly heavy weights for use in rivers, or if the weather is stormy. It is difficult to suggest a specific carrying weight because this depends very much on the water's character.

A beautiful barbel is a great prize for any angler.

Tench are very cautious fish. That's why silence is important where you are fishing.

For small, shallow lakes on calm days with no wind, I suggest floats that carry two to six grammes of weight. If it is windy or there is a current (as in a river), they should carry more weight. This is true for fixed floats, as well.

The slip float

If you fish in water that is deeper than three metres or if you want to cast over a long distance, you will have to use a slip float that runs freely along the line. In this situation, use floats that are as light as possible. This float will then serve as a very reliable bite indicator.

Let us proceed to the rig: if you decide to fish with a slip-float, the first thing to put on your line is the stopper. There are several ways to do this, but for beginners I strongly recommend a simple rubber band. It is easiest to fix this "stop knot" to the main line. Once your stop knot is attached you'll have to add a rubber stop bead and, after that, the float. This way, the bead that is held by the stop knot will stop the float and thus the rig reaches the perfect water depth. From here on in, everything is the same as for a fixed float: tying on the swivel, weighting, and attaching the ready-made leader. Depth fathoming also works very much the same way, except that your sinker has to be considerably heavier to pull your float under water. To change the length of your rig, you don't have to move the float but instead the rubber band that functions as a stop knot. The angling, too, is fairly similar to the method described above.

However, it is hardly possible to throw maize or maggots very far by hand. If you're angling at a distance, you'll have to rely on a few tricks and devices: catapults and open-ended or blockend feeders. I recommend the blockend feeder, which will equip you to cast any chum up to about forty metres. Another advantage is that casting a blockend feeder is learned very easily—two or three practice shots are usually all you need.

In this fishing situation, too, it is a good idea to start fishing on the bottom and change the depth if you are not successful. Fishing with a float is certainly the best method when you angle for non-predatory fish, but there are also good rigs for ground fishing. I will tell you about those very shortly.

Legering

Most large non-predatory fish are caught near the bottom. Naturally, there are exceptions, but these serve to prove the rule. Because of the heavier weight of both the sinkers and the fish, I recommend a line of at least 0.30 millimetres for ground fishing. The hooks can also be larger: sizes 2 to 8 are the ones I'd suggest. These hook and leader combinations are available as prefabricated leaders.

Legering has a lot of things going for it. The strongest argument is certainly the feeding. If you want to ensure your success you should go out to feed the fish about two days before you actually fish at the spot. This allows the fish to get used to the food—they are not only encouraged to feed there, but also get used to the type of food you're offering, even conditioned to it.

Once the fish get used to the fact that there is food in a certain spot, there is no longer any reason to fish above the bottom or even in the open water. Instead, make sure that your bait also comes to rest on the ground. In order to do that you should use a sufficiently heavy weight, called a sinker. You can also use a weighted swim feeder. The swim feeder makes sure that there is additional food near the bait on your hook and attracts even more fish.

Feeding

If you start a long-term feeding campaign, you should definitely present your hook and bait at the bottom. This can be done with the help of sinkers or swim feeders. Swim feeders are an additional attraction for the fish.

The rule, "As light as possible, as heavy as necessary" is true for

This angler uses a typical rest while fishing with his leger rod.

Yummy—a filled swim feeder. This must taste good to the fish, mustn't it!

ground fishing, too. In this case it means that the sinker should be just heavy enough to keep the bait down near the ground. This depends on the weather as well as the type of water. For fishing in a small lake on a calm day with no wind, a sinker of 10 to 30 grammes will be sufficient. If there are waves or if you fish in a river, the sinker needs to be somewhat heavier.

There are several types of weights that can be used for this kind of fishing. The only thing that really matters is that you can thread it onto the main line. Some weights have a hole in the middle so that they can run along the line; depending on their shape, these weights are called bullet sinkers, egg sinkers, or barrels. There are also weights with eyelets that can be attached to a snap lock swivel with a bit of silicone or plastic tubing. This method is highly recommended for fishing on muddy water beds: a self-supporting sinker (such as used in a pop-up rig) will embed its heavy lower end in the mud while its air-filled tube rises upright against the current, allowing the line to run freely through the eyelet on top without getting caught in the mud.

If you anticipate frequent bites from tench, carp and barbel you should use what is called a bait-walker rig. You will have to attach a stopper and bead to the line in front of the weight. As a result, when the fish swims forward a few centimetres it will push the weight against the stopper, called the boom. This pushes the hook deeper into the mouth of the fish and when you set the hook you will only rarely miss. But it is most important that you put a pearl between the weight and the swivel, which has to be fastened with a clinch knot. This pearl protects the knot from the weight or the tube because the weight or sinker push quite hard against the swivel while casting the line and playing the fish.

Swim feeders come in a variety of forms. For example, some are open at both ends and some are only open on one end. There are some with eyelets so that the line can run through them freely, while others are hooked into the snap swivel or a side leader. If you mount a swim feeder as a side leader I suggest that you loop it in—so I have provided you with a few detailed drawings of the knots required here. Unless it is attached to a side leader, the swim feeder is attached in the same way as a normal sinker.

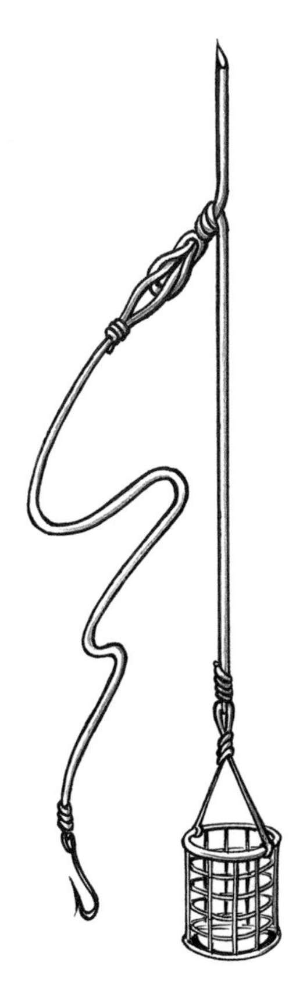

Swim feeder on a side leader.

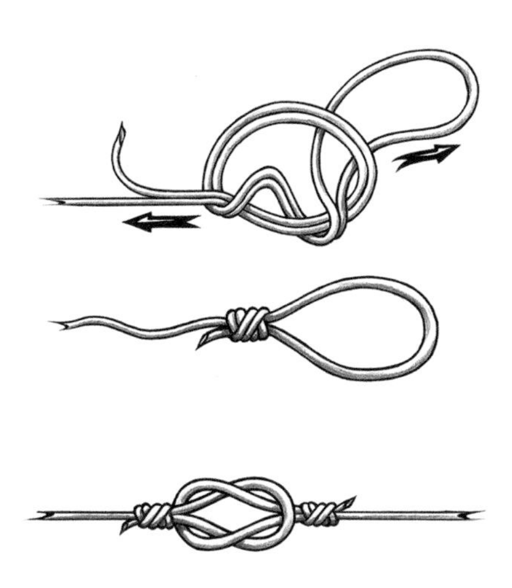

The surgeon's loop or double loop and the interlocking of two loops.

The swim feeder to attract the fish, the maggots to hook them.

Chum

A mixture that has proven reliable can be made of one third breadcrumbs, one third fishmeal, and one third cornmeal. There should also be some particles in the chum, which can be maize kernels, hemp seeds, or maggots.

Feeding always works the same way when you angle for non-predatory fish. If you use a swim feeder you should enrich any feed made of maize and breadcrumbs with maggots and the like. And of course there are many other possible additives such as hemp seed or wheat grains, fishmeal or maize flower. The chum must be very solid so that it can be pressed into the swim feeder without falling out of the basket or openings when you cast. Since you can reach enormous distances when casting a sinker, I suggest you use the feeding aids mentioned above, especially the catapult.

Of course, you can use your general-purpose rod when ground fishing for non-predatory fish and—certainly to begin with—I would recommend this without reservation. However, you will need a rod rest to support your rod while angling this way (this rod rest can be either a tripod or a sandspike). Now pull some of the line down and hang some silver paper or something similar over the line to function as a bite indicator. You can also buy little gadgets made for this purpose.

However, if you find yourself doing a lot of legering or enjoying it so much that you do it regularly, you will want to invest in a leger rod. This has to do with bite indication during ground fishing. For this kind of angling, the best bite indicator is the tip of the rod—which is why this tip has to be extremely fine and sensitive. At the same time, though, you'll have to cast quite heavy weights. Leger rods are therefore designed to have a strong "backbone" for the casting and playing, as well as exchangeable swinging and quivering tips as bite indicators. As soon as the tip bows and stays down, the fish should be hooked.

Sinkers

There are many different kinds of sinkers. If they have a hole through the middle they are designed to ride on the line. A typical example of that kind of weight is the classic coffin weight. All other sinkers are equipped with an eye and can be snapped onto the line by their eye.

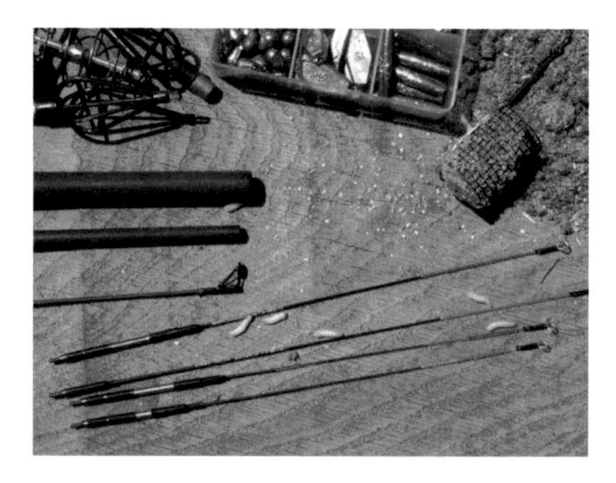

Quiver tips in different thicknesses.

Equipment for Modern Carp Fishing

No other fishing speciality has developed as rapidly during recent years as carp fishing. Almost every year a new record is broken, and the carp has become the most popular angling quarry all over Europe. Photographs of happy fishermen holding an enormous fish in their hands certainly make hearts beat faster. Many a young angler only earns his or her fishing license so as to be free to hunt for a fat carp. I don't find this a particularly healthy development, since I think every future fisherman should start by trying to outwit a few roach and the like, but I'm afraid there is no way to stop the revolution. That is why I have allocated considerable space to carp fishing in this book.

Of course, you can always fish for carp with the general-purpose rod I have described above, and again that is the advisable thing to do. But here I will describe the equipment you need if you aspire to a really big carp—that is, a fish weighing between 10 and 50 pounds! For this kind of fishing you will need a dedicated carp rod. This angling specialisation was actually developed in Britain, so the English technical terms are used internationally. A carp rod should have a length of 11 to 13 feet, or approximately 3.30 to 3.90 metres. Carp rods are not measured by casting weight, but rather by test curves that are given in English pound values (lbs). Carp rods typically have test curves of 2 to 3.5 lbs, which corresponds to a casting weight of 50 to 90 grammes.

Landing a big carp is a genuine challenge. This is why fishing for carp is becoming increasingly popular.

Carp rods have very strong spines, but are still through-action rods that allow long-distance casting. Furthermore, they offer enough flexibility to play the hooked fish as it fights to escape. If you should decide to take up with carp fishing, I recommend your first carp rod have a length of 12 feet and a test curve of 2.5 lbs. With this rod you should be able to deal with almost any

Playing a carp calls for relaxed muscles and a calm mind—despite your feverish excitement.

Carp rods

Your general-purpose rod should be versatile enough to use for some carp fishing as well. But those who wish to specialise in carp fishing will want to use a carp rod. A good model measures 12 feet in length and has a testing curve of 2.5 lbs.

Fishing for carp works best with an elastic monofilament line.

situation you might encounter while angling.

There are also factors to be taken into consideration regarding your choice of reel and line. For carp fishing, large fixed reels with baitrunners have become the norm. The baitrunner is a lever at the back of the reel whose purpose is to counteract the drag control. This allows the fish to take off with a lot of line after it has taken the hook. As soon as the fisherman or fisherwoman uses the crank of the reel, the baitrunner stops working and the drag control sets in again. Since a large, vigorously fighting carp can take up to a hundred metres of line from your spool in the course of a drill, you will need to use a spool that has capacity for about 300 metres of 0.35 millimetre line.

Most carp anglers tend to use a classic pod to hold their rods.

So let's proceed to the line. The diameter of your line should be no less than 0.35 millimetres. I strongly suggest that you stick with a monofilament line. Certainly, you may encounter a few anglers out there who swear by braided line for carp fishing, but I don't think this is a good idea at all! Let me explain briefly: one feature of braided line is its extremely low flexibility. But it is precisely this feature that is essential for any line used for carp fishing. Imagine: at the end of your line, approximately 100 metres away, is a 25-pound carp putting up a terrific fight. The distance alone means you will lose a lot of "feel" for the fish. That forces you to rely on the flexibility of the line as an additional buffer, otherwise there is a real danger that the hook will cut itself right out of the fish's mouth.

Lines used for carp fishing

When fishing for carp, I strongly recommend using a monofilament line. Its superior elasticity is a great help when you play the fish, exhausting it more easily. The size should be no less than 0.35 millimetres.

The baitrunner reel has become the norm for carp fishing. A simple shifting of a lever turns off the drag control.

The bolt rig has turned out to be a revolutionary invention. How does it work? To keep it as simple as possible, the bolt rig builds on two features: firstly, there is the baited hook on the so-called hook link, and secondly there is the sinker which is attached to the main line. The hook link exploits the feeding habits of the carp. As described earlier, the carp "inhales" its food to find out whether it is edible. Therefore, the bait is attached to a hair-thin line right next to the hook. The carp pulls in the bait and at the same time inadvertently picks up the hook. If the carp notices its mistake, it tries to spit out the bait, which instantly causes the hook to embed itself lightly in the carp's mouth. As a result, the carp bolts and swims against the sinker, which unavoidably sets the hook in its mouth.

I will now describe the rig in detail. Today, you can also buy prefabricated leaders for the hook link apparatus. These ready-made rigs will do very well to start with, but sooner or later, all carp anglers will end up making their own rigs. I have therefore included a detailed drawing of the no-knot knot here (see illustration on page 54), which is most commonly used on the bolt rig.

Let's start with the hook: use hooks sized 2 to 6 and make sure that they are really sharp. Be absolutely sure to tie the leader to a barrel swivel without a snap. The snap is not only the weak element in the rig, but it also threatens to cause tangles while you cast.

But how do you get the weight fixed firmly to the main line? Let me show you two possible ways to do that. The first is by using an in-line weight (this means the line is running through the weight itself). At the end of the weight is a long rubber tube into which you pull the swivel of the leader and the weight is firmly attached. The other possibility works in a very similar manner: for this one, you use a short plastic tube. A clip fixed to this short tube lets you attach the weight. Again, you pull the swivel into the tube and thus fix on the weight. This way of fixing the weight is called the safety rig because it ensures that the fish will manage to get rid of the weight if the line breaks.

If you fish this way you should use a very heavy sinker to make sure that the bolt rig really works and the hook gets firmly lodged. Use weights of between 90 and 200 grammes: 90 grammes should suffice in a lake with no waves, larger lakes or rivers will require you to use a somewhat heavier weight. Furthermore, carp anglers tend to use a long tube with a diameter of about one milli-

The security rig: the weight is mounted on a little plastic piece and thus falls off if the line rips or gets stuck.

metre. The main line runs through this tube, which is then attached directly to the weight or to the short plastic tube. The purpose of the long tube is to avoid tangles while casting, which is why it has to be somewhat longer than the

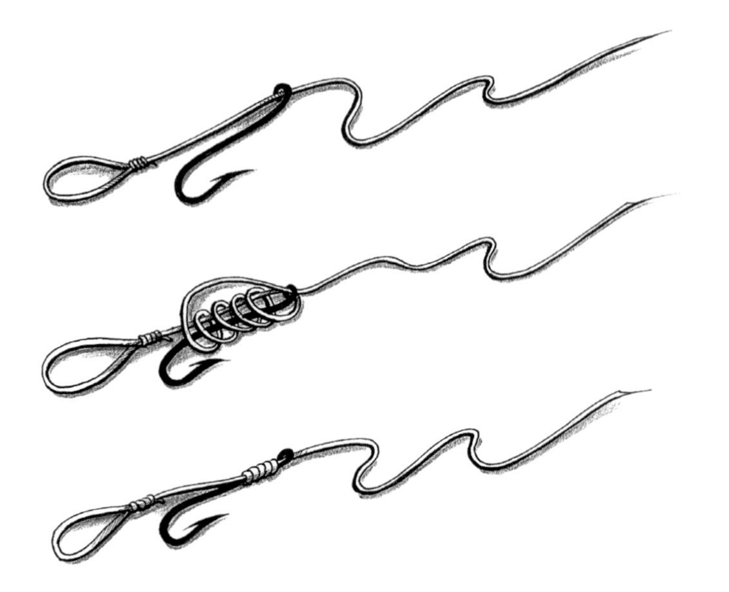

This "no-knot" knot is used to attach the hook to the leader when fishing for carp.

The bolt rig

With the correct rig you can make sure that the fish gets on the hook without your having to strike it. For a bolt rig, choose a weight that is not too light; it should weigh at least 90 grammes.

leader. The leader can then slide over the tube without becoming tangled. The leader itself should measure around 25 centimetres.

In modern carp fishing, many people prefer to use an electronic bite indicator. While there is no need for you to rush off instantly to get one of these gadgets for your own tackle box, in the long run, there may be no way around it.

You will know a carp has bitten when line is pulled off your reel. Since fishing for carp is a definite challenge to your patience you will have to watch your rod, even if you are fishing with an indicator hanging from your line. But you can imagine how the story will end: the bite will inevitably happen at the exact moment you finally take your eyes off the rod. And believe me, every second that carp will take more line off your reel and within a few heartbeats will have found a safe spot from which you will only very rarely be able to extract it. However, if your rod rests on an electronic bite indicator, it will start beeping as soon as the line is pulled—and that's one bite you certainly won't miss!

Electronic bite indicators are symbolic of the technological developments being made in angling.

Feeding and Waiting

The number one carp bait is the boilie, which was developed in England—where else? It consists of different kinds of flour, egg and other ingredients that are kneaded, rolled into balls and then boiled (hence its name). This form of bait comes ready-made and can be bought anywhere. Many carp fishermen, however, prefer to prepare their boilies themselves, so I will outline briefly how that is done—more than that would take us beyond the scope of this book.

If you want to prepare your own boilies you will need special tools. Especially important are the rolling table and the dough gun. The rolling table is a tool that consists of two grooved plastic panels. Squeeze the dough through the dough gun to form a long sausage and lay it onto the two panels. Then press the panels together and hey presto: boilies. The dough gun resembles a silicone syringe used by plumbers to caulk corners and cracks. To knead the dough I prefer to use a strong electric drill. Naturally, you can also prepare it by hand, but don't forget that it has to have the consistency of stiff bread dough. If you prepare the boilie dough by hand you may have some muscle pain afterwards.

It is highly advisable to feed from a boat because you can lure the fish to the area where you cast your bait. However, this is not permitted everywhere.

The dry ingredients for the preparation of boilies are fishmeal, soy flour, nut flour, birdfeed and diverse kinds of dried milk. There are a whole range of possible additional ingredients, but it is better to start simple. The liquid items are egg, sweetener, artificial fla-

A slim mirror carp from a lake. This is rare because lake-dwelling mirror carp tend to be built on massive lines.

Boilies—the carp bait

The boilie has become the number one bait for carp. Nowadays you can choose from a large variety of commercial boilies in addition to homemade dough balls. These boilies are almost all of very good quality and their cost is not prohibitive.

A boilie recipe

I recommend this recipe for a way to initially attract carp: the banana nut boilie.

350 grammes nut flour
250 grammes soy flour
200 grammes birdfeed
100 grammes semolina
100 grammes lactalbumin
15 millilitres sweetener
20 millilitres banana flavouring
10 eggs

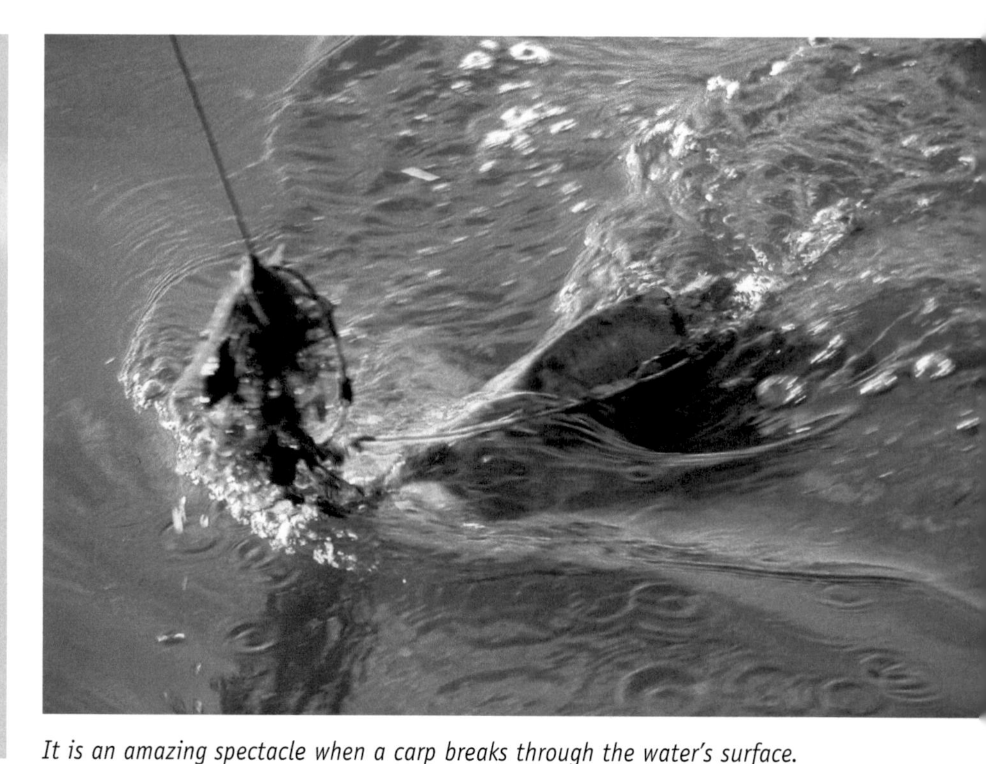

It is an amazing spectacle when a carp breaks through the water's surface.

vour, and possibly preservatives. You will need approximately ten eggs per kilogramme of dry mix.

Mix the dry ingredients first, then mix the wet ingredients separately. Now combine the wet and dry ingredients and knead thoroughly. As mentioned above, the dough should have a very firm consistency. As soon as the dough no longer sticks to your fingers, it is ready. Now pack it slowly into the dough gun and squeeze into long sausages. Convert the sausages to boilies, as explained above.

Preparing boilies is a lot of fun. All you need is a rolling table and a dough gun.

But you are not finished yet—the boilie balls you now have are still raw. They must be boiled for about three minutes. It is impossible to give an exact time: just watch for the balls to rise to the surface. When they do, take them out of the water. The boilies should be dried for a minimum of 24 hours; then they are ready for use.

The number two carp bait is particles. Particles covers all sorts of bait that consists of grains, such as maize, hemp, tiger nuts and the like. Since you will certainly need maize when you fish for carp, either for feeding or as bait, it is worth your while to buy a bag of feed maize. Feed maize is less expensive, and its grains are larger and harder than those of canned maize. Apart from that, its larger size will attract fewer small fish. All types of bait, be it boilies, maize or tiger nut, are threaded onto the hair rig and held with a dedicated stopper.

Feeding is an indispensable part of carp fishing—as necessary as water is for boiling noodles. Again, the fish need to be accustomed to a certain spot and food type. So whatever you plan to bait your hook with should also be offered as feed ahead of time.

Be sure to take the season into account when you fish for carp. During the cold season, their metabolism slows and they therefore feed less. Let's start with spring: the colder the weather in spring the less you should feed. During spring you should definitely have particles among your feeds. I usually use a feed mix of bread crumbs, maize flour, hemp flour, and a large part of feed maize. Do make a point of soaking the feed maize in water for 24 hours and then boiling it before use. If you do not do this, the maize kernels will swell in the fish's stomach and cause considerable and unnecessary pain. I like to roll the feed into tennis-ball-sized spheres and freeze them. By the following day, those frozen balls can be tossed more than 50 metres with your catapult or scoop. I also add some boilies to the feed mix because I always use them to bait at least one rod.

In summer I only feed boilies, especially since by then the fish should be used to the spot. When feeding in summer, note the weather. When it gets too hot the carps will stop eating again. You can feed a lot in mild summer weather; when it is hot, feed less.

Autumn is a heavy feeding time for carps. Somehow, the fish seem to notice that winter is approaching and fill up well in preparation. You can count on substantial catches during a mild autumn, and that also means you can feed basically as much as you please. But do stay within reasonable limits: I have seen people going to their club lakes daily and throwing in ten kilogrammes of feed. This is not only completely unnecessary, but even harmful: the quality of the

A large common or king carp caught in a river.

Granddad, dad, daughter and the fish: angling is something the entire family can enjoy.

Feeding carp

When feeding carp it's important to take into account the season and the weather. Carp reduce their metabolism during cold spells and therefore they eat less. The same is true for hot spells during summer. For the angler this means feeding only sparingly during extremely hot or very cold times. Autumn, on the other hand, is the time of year when carps eat with relish.

water deteriorates since all that is not eaten will rot.

Feed only very sparingly in winter. If you happen to know exactly where the fish roam it is even preferable to fish without feeding, using only a baited hook. One thing is certain: the myth of the evasive winter carp is long outdated. If you know where the fish are you can also catch them during winter.

When you have prepared your spot well by feeding and have set out your bait, the wait begins. Your rods should be arranged so that the line enters the water as soon as possible to keep it from drifting in the wind. However, if you fish in overgrown areas or in a river, your rod should be very upright so that as little line as possible is actually in the water.

Now all you need is a lot of patience while you wait. Enjoy these moments. There is hardly a better time to enjoy nature than while you fish for carp—at least until the flurry of beeping makes you jump and grab for your rod.

Tackle for Catching Predatory Fish

The pike is the most popular of all predatory fish. Every angler probably dreams of catching a really big pike at least once in his or her life. But zander, the secret predator, and eel, the mysterious snake-shaped fish, are also prized quarry for every fisherman. As always, there are many things to consider when selecting the bait and equipment for your forays in quest of predatory fish.

Without question, the number one bait when you intend to fish for predators is the baitfish. That means before you can set out to catch your real quarry you will have to catch the bait—you have already learned how to do that in the chapter on non-predatory fish. Ideal baitfish are roach, bream, bass or bleak. If you are not in a position to angle for your baitfish they are also available for purchase. My own preference is to catch a large quantity of baitfish and then freeze them for future use.

A large pike is a challenge for any angler.

Though one occasionally hears objections that frozen baitfish are not as attractive to predatory fish as fresh ones, this has not been my experience.

In order to fish for predatory fish you will need some additional equipment. First and foremost you must have artificial bait: spoons and spinners, wobblers and plugs. What these kinds of artificial bait look like and how you use them is explained later, in the chapter on spin fishing.

Apart from that, it is always advisable to take what is called a pike gag. When you try to remove the hook from the mouth of a pike there is a serious risk of getting badly hurt by some of its 700 teeth. And while we are on the subject of pike teeth, I strongly advise you to always use a steel leader when angling for predators. For your own protection, don't be slack about this, even when you only intend to fish for a zander: a pike won't realise that is your intention and it might grab the bait first.

Steel leaders can be bought but I would encourage you to try your hand at making your own. When you fish for predators you should make every effort to use the most appropriate materials and decide for yourself the best length for your leader. Ready-made leaders tend to be on the short side. Imagine—if a one-metre pike swallows your 25-centimetre roach, it will very quickly reach the end of your 40, 50, or 60-centimetre leader. And believe me, you won't get a giant like that hooked again any time soon!

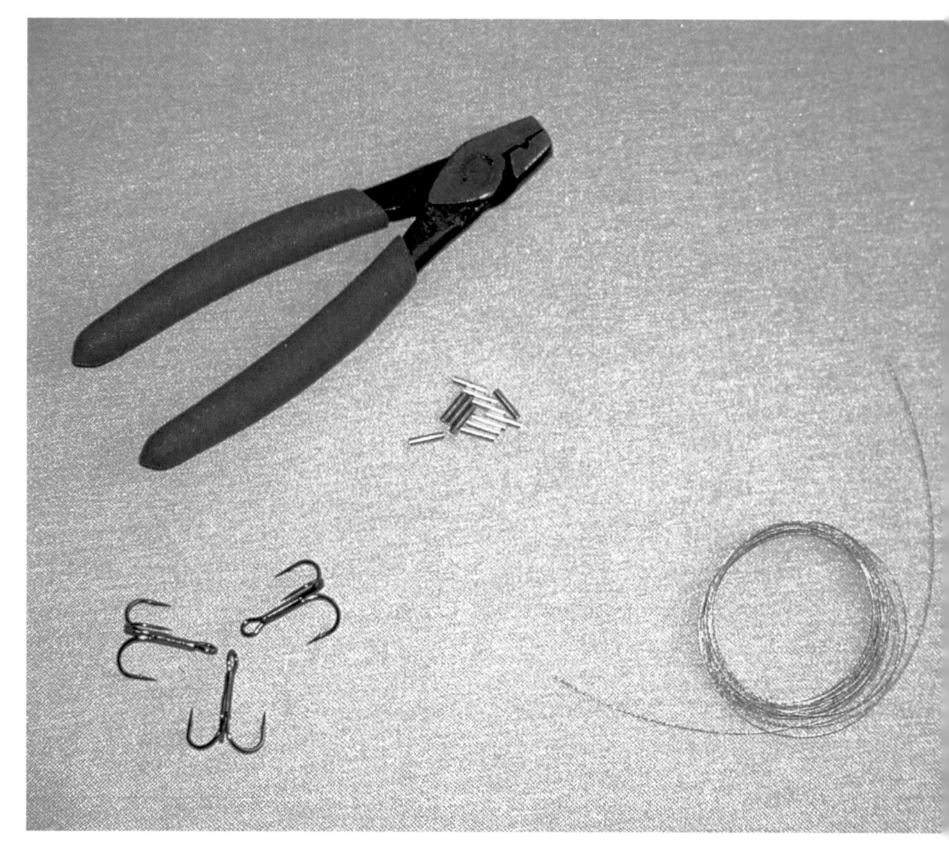

These are the materials you need to make a steel leader.

So instead, buy steel line by the metre and use 49-strand wire. This means that the cable consists of 49 separate fine steel filaments, which makes the leader very soft and supple. Apart from that you need crimping sleeves and pliers. Naturally, you can't forget the hook. For a normal steel leader I suggest a number 1 hook.

What follows are step-by-step instructions for making a steel or wire leader (see the picture sequence on the following page). To begin, cut off a piece of the right length from your roll of steel wire. If you plan on fishing with a dead baitfish I would generally suggest a length of about 90 centimetres to give you a leader about 80 centimetres long.

Step one: slip the leader wire through the crimping sleeve.

Step two: make a loop and slip the end of the steel line back through the crimping sleeve.

Step three: to make sure the loop will hold, pass the

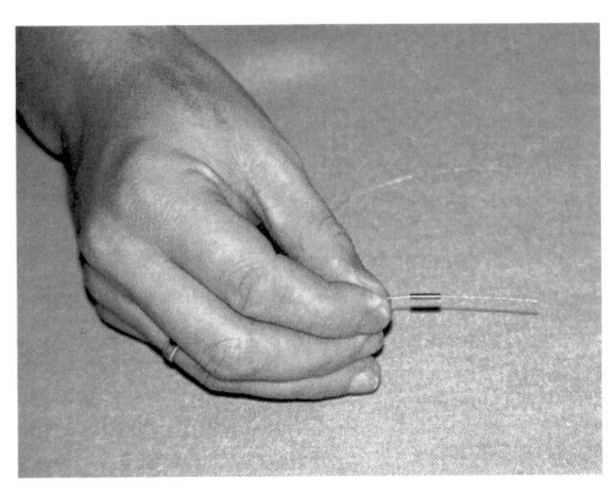

Step one: the leader wire is slipped through the crimping sleeve.

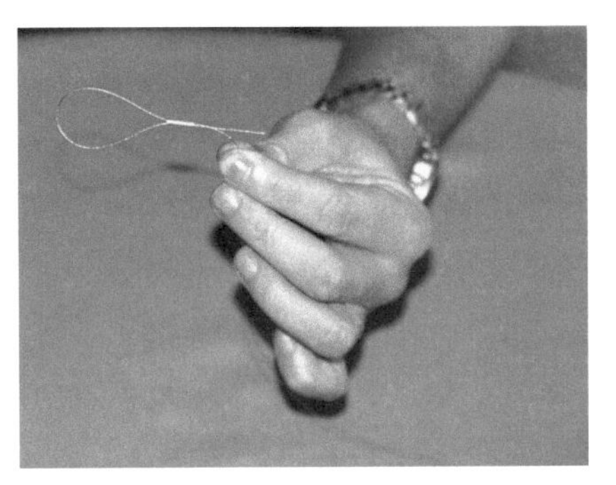

Step two: form a loop and pass the line back through the crimping sleeve.

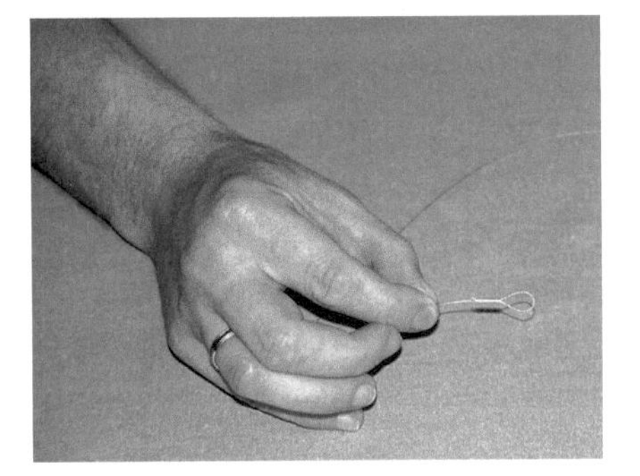

Step three: to reinforce it, thread the line through the crimping sleeve a third time.

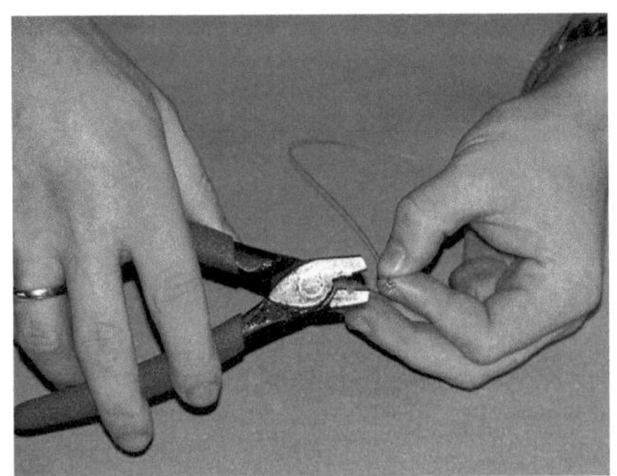

Step four: the crimping sleeve is flattened with pliers.

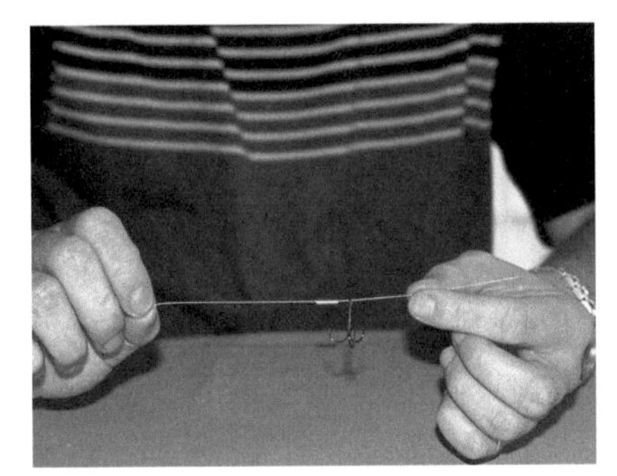

Step five: now repeat all these steps at the other end of the leader, except this time the line is threaded through the crimping sleeve and a treble hook.

line through the crimping sleeve a third time.

Step four: if the loop is the size you desire and there isn't too much extra material sticking out of the crimping sleeve, use the pliers to flatten the sleeve.

Step five: slip the other end of the leader through a second crimping sleeve and through the eye of a treble hook.

Step six: now continue as for the other end of the leader. Form a loop, slip the line through the crimping sleeve again, pass it through the crimping sleeve for the third time and flatten the sleeve with pliers.

And there you are: your first finished leader, made with your own hands!

You can—with just a few reservations—fish for any kind of predatory fish with your general-purpose rod. However, if you should develop a knack for spin fishing, you will probably end up purchasing a light but strong rod, in order to avoid the recurring muscle pain caused by continual throwing out and reeling in of your rig. While you're at it, you can choose a smaller spool for this rod since you will need a lot less line than for other kinds of angling.

But to start with, your general-purpose rod will do well for you with baitfish as well as with artificial bait. When fishing for predatory fish, though, I strongly suggest you take along at least one back-up spool with braided line since this kind of line is clearly designed for the demands of spin fishing.

Let me explain that briefly: when you spin fish, you pull the bait through the water in order to make the bait move in such a way as to entice an alert predatory fish to follow the bait and then to swallow it. In this situation, the lack of stretch in the line becomes an advantage because the bait moves, then the predator snaps it up, and the line resists. These three elements usually ensure that the fish hooks itself. Furthermore, braided line can be cast better and further which means that you can fish a much larger area.

Fishing with Natural Bait

There are many different predatory fish to be found in our waters. Obviously, there are specific techniques for each kind of fish. But you may still catch a zander when you angle for eel, or a pike may take the hook you cast to catch a zander. I will limit myself to the three predatory fish that are most frequently fished in Europe: on the following pages you will learn how best to catch pike, zander and eel using natural bait.

Pike can be caught with float rigs, and also by ground fishing with a sinker. Let me begin with the float rig. As far as the rig is concerned, fishing for pike with a float rig works in much the same way as fishing for non-predatory fish with a float. But you need to remember that the baitfish weighs quite a lot more than (for example) grains of maize. This is why you should use a float capable of carrying a fair amount of weight: 10 grammes is the absolute minimum, 20 or 40 grammes is even better. This also means you will need more weight on your float.

I suggest you use a fairly large bullet or egg-shaped sinker with a hole through the middle; in addition to that you will need some split shot lead.

A beautiful pike like this is without doubt the high point of a successful day's angling!

Even small pike eat roach that are quite large. Make sure you always keep the applicable size limits in mind.

The principle that I outlined above for the other rigs applies here, as well: the largest weight should be directly underneath the float—in this case the bullet or egg-shaped sinker—followed by the split shot in order by size. The swivel should be correspondingly large; number 4 is an acceptable size, and number 2 is better still. Always use snap swivels because it is a very time-consuming and tedious task to change the leader without a snap. I have already written about the steel leader. But let me reiterate: never fish for pike without a rig that includes a steel leader!

When fishing for pike, you should try to use only whole baitfish that are at least 15 centimetres long. The roach is probably the most popular baitfish for pike. Let me explain exactly how to attach the roach to your leader so that it serves as attractive bait: first pierce the roach's side with a bait needle directly below the dorsal fin. Then hook the steel leader to the needle and pull it all the way through the roach. Finally, anchor your treble hook in the gills area of the roach, and there you are!

You probably don't need reminding to fathom out the depth of your fishing spot before you start angling, so all you need to know now is where to find the pike. The general rule that the bait should be somewhere close to the bottom holds true here, too. In the section on the feeding habits of fish, however, I pointed out that the location of the pike's mouth at the top of its head indicates that it tends to take its prey from beneath. Therefore it is always a good idea to offer the baitfish a half metre or even a metre above the bottom. Especially in summer, when there is less oxygen in the lower strata of water, pike can be found in the upper regions of the water.

Big pike come out in particular when the weather is bad.

But since, generally speaking, pike can often be found close to the bottom, you can use the legering technique. This is even more advisable if you've set your sights on one of the particularly large specimens. In this case it is best to attach the sinker to a plastic tube which allows the line to run through. If the bottom is muddy use a pop-up rig, otherwise just use a weight that is heavy enough to get your rig to the bottom. If you decide to try ground fishing, the baitfish may also be a tad larger. Don't hesitate to use a 20-centimetre roach. A huge fish like this, however, should be attached to the leader with two treble hooks. For this rig, pierce the baitfish in the tail area with the bait needle and pull the leader through. The first treble hook is embedded in the gill area, the second in the flank of the baitfish.

Fishing for pike

Pike are known to go for large baitfish, roach being the most frequently used. No matter what kind you use, pierce the swim bladder of the baitfish, otherwise it will drift off towards the surface and cancel out the depth of the rig. Pike can usually be found close to the bottom. Especially during summer, however, you might have to hunt for them in the higher strata of the water.

With this set-up, I would suggest an electronic bite indicator. When ground fishing for pike, loosen the drag on the reel a great deal, and even open the bail, so that the pike can take as much line as it needs. Here again, the best thing would be a reel with a baitrunner lever. Since pike can reach a length of more than one metre, you should use a line of at least 0.35 millimetres.

The best time to fish for pike is definitely dawn. Although they tend to have a second meal at dusk, they are out for a much shorter period then. In the autumn, though, you can try for pike anytime on rainy days.

Angling for zander is much like fishing for pike, but the rig can be somewhat lighter for zander. Because the zander's mouth is a lot smaller than that of the pike, the baitfish you offer to the zander will be considerably smaller than those

An enormous zander—a fish like this isn't caught very often.

used for pike, and thus lighter. Choose baitfish no longer than 15 centimetres—and they may certainly be shorter! Baitfish cut into smallish pieces are ideal. Halved fish work best, no matter whether you use the head or the tail piece. Other parts, such as the side of a large bream, are also options.

The need for lighter weight holds true both for fishing with floats and for legering. You can use lighter floats when you fish for zander, as a lighter weight will be sufficient to keep your bait near the bottom. Consequently, the main line can also be somewhat lighter, although I would still advise against using any line thinner than 0.30 millimetres.

It is worth your while to fish for zander in the course of the night. That's the time when these fish hunt close to the shore.

You need a particular type of hook when angling for zander. Most people use double hooks: one hook is free to pierce the mouth of the zander, while the other hook is used to attach the baitfish. There are also ready-made leaders on the market specifically for zander fishing. But these are made of mono line and I would discourage you from using them. Just stick to leaders made with steel line. The modern 49-strand lines are so supple and elastic that they work well for zander and can still resist a pike if it accidentally gets onto your hook. In addition, there are also Kevlar leaders. These are a good alternative since they stay inconspicuous and manage to resist even a pike—at least for a while. Only if you fish in a lake or river that is absolutely free of pike would I advise you to use mono line leaders. Otherwise really do stick to steel leaders.

I keep stressing this point for a single reason. A cruel habit has become common in recent years: people are fishing with very light material as if their many losses are negligible. Always remember that if your line is severed, it involves more than just a loss of material—it condemns a living creature to swim around for the rest of its life with your line dragging from its mouth.

Zander can be caught at any time, but they bite most frequently in the early morning, the late evening and at night. Especially during the night, zander like to come close to the shore to hunt. When you fish for zander it is essential to give the fish enough line; this applies equally to float fishing and legering. Still, zander are extremely sensitive and that means you must keep your bail

The result of a night angling for eel: three eels and a carp.

open. Even the light drag of a reel with a very good bait-runner can make the zander suspicious and cause it to spit its prey back out.

People tell the most mysterious stories about eels; the truth content of these stories often seems minimal to non-existent. It is true, however, that eels are amazing survival artists. If absolutely necessary, eels are able to cross dry land in order to get from one body of water to another. This is highly unusual, though! Don't hold your breath hoping to find a "flock of eels" while out walking, just waiting for you to collect them in a bag!

Eels also have an extraordinarily keen olfactory sense. Biologists have discovered that an eel can still detect an aroma if a thimblefull of essence is dissolved in the water of a lake 100 times bigger than Lake Windermere! This extraordinary ability obviously has direct consequences for us anglers because the fish can detect if you were smoking before baiting your hook or if you stopped to refill your car with petrol on your way to the lake or river. You should definitely try to avoid these kinds of activities when you plan on angling for eel.

Fishing for eel is quite similar to angling for pike and zander. But you will have to use even lighter material for eel than you do for zander. In calm water you can even use very fine, fixed floats if the depth of the water allows it. If you prefer legering for eel I suggest that you use light coffin weights. Coffin weights are hexagonal-shaped weights that are pierced through the centre. They have the advantage of lying firmly on the ground while the line passes through them without rolling off. If the bottom is muddy, I again suggest that you use a pop-up rig, but make sure it is light enough.

The only bait I can suggest for eel is night crawlers. I have told you that large eels with wide heads do feed on small fish, but if you use fish for bait you will have to use a steel leader, which would drastically lessen your chances of catching an eel. Worms have

Angling for zander

For zander you will need smaller bait than for pike. If you use an entire baitfish it should be no longer than 10 to 15 centimetres, but you can use cut-up baitfish as well. If night fishing is allowed where you angle, it is worth trying to catch zander from the shore during the night. Zander are extremely cautious, so you should always open your bail when fishing for them.

another advantage as well: they are the best bait there is for eels. Statistically, eels take hooks baited with night crawlers a lot more often than hooks baited with small fish. On a humid, dark summer night I can almost guarantee you a catch if you use night crawlers. As far as the hook is concerned I recommend the commercial leaders specially designed for eels. Their hooks are quite large. A number 4 hook should handle any eel that you might catch.

Eels are without question night hunters. These fish like darkness so much that even a clear night with a full moon will quite noticeably reduce your chances of a bite. Your main line should not be too thin, since eels that are played typically try to reach obstacles. If they manage to reach one they curl around it and this will easily break your line. It follows that you need to put a lot of pressure on the eel right after the hit. I recommend a 0.30-millimetre line.

Fishing for eel

Eels are nocturnal fish; the night hours are the best time to angle for them. If you fish with floats, use a light that can be attached to your pole float with cellotape or something similar. Or you can equip yourself with a dedicated night float. With a night float, you can insert a light into the transparent antenna as needed. The night float is also the float of choice when you try to catch zander during the night.

Sheatfish and eel prefer to feed during the night and both love night crawlers.

It makes sense to go spin fishing at dawn or dusk, times when all predatory fish are hunting.

Spin Fishing

The term "spin fishing" derives from one of the artificial baits used for it, the spinner, although the term also refers to an active way of angling with artificial bait in general. Spin fishing requires that you be not only very active, but also extremely flexible. This means you should take as little tackle as possible with you to the shore. The rod and net in your hands, and a small backpack containing various baits and other small necessities are all you really need. These necessities have been discussed before: a tape measure, a hanging balance, a priest and a knife. Equipped in this way, you can move about long stretches of any water body and fish where you like. The lake that belongs to my club, for example, measures about 16 acres. It takes me about three hours to fish the entire lake and I rarely come home without having caught a predatory fish.

There are many different kinds of artificial bait. They can be roughly categorised according to the material they are made of. Spoons and spinners are made of sheet metal, while plugs are typically made of wood, or today of plastic. All kinds of lures such as wobblers and rubber fish, including twisters, are often made of rubber.

Spoons typically have a very simple design. They consist of a piece of sheet metal that has been given a very specific shape. The front and back end of the metal piece are pierced and equipped with a snap ring. Attached to the snap ring at the rear end is a treble hook, while the snap ring at the front end serves to attach the bait device to the leader. The curving of the metal causes the spoon to move erratically when it is pulled through the water. This leads predatory fish to believe they are dealing with a small fish that is hurt and thus

Different kinds of artificial bait. At the top from left to right: spoon, spinner, plug, rubber fish; at the bottom a large rubber fish.

easy prey. Spoons come in all sizes and weights, depending on how fast they sink to the bottom, how far they are cast and what kind of predatory fish they are intended for.

The spinner works in a very similar way, except the curved metal sheet is only pierced at one end. Typically, a central shaft, a piece of strong wire, is put through the hole and attached to its end is a single or treble hook. If you pull the lure through the water, the metal sheet (called the blade or vane) begins to rotate around the central bar. This creates an effect that is visually striking, but also sends out throbbing pressure waves. The predatory fish pick up the pressure waves via the pores in their lateral line and are thus induced to bite. These lures, of course, can also be bought in any conceivable size.

Wobblers or plugs are availablein all sizes and all colours. Typically, they try to recreate the natural colouring of the fish they imitate. Don't be surprised if you come across a plug that looks like a pike: pike often eat younger fish of their own species. Various plugs are designed to reach different depths. This depends on the diving vane or lip attached to the head of the lure: the flatter the vane, the deeper the plug will dive. Nowadays, you can also find floating plugs that originated in North America. These plugs have no vane in order to allow them to swim along the surface of the water. This is especially helpful during summer months, for example to fish in fields of water lilies where diving plugs would get caught in the plants. If you are lucky enough to see a pike rise from the depths like a submarine and snatch a floating plug on the surface, it's an awesome spectacle!

Rubber fish and twisters are the most up-to-date lures. They revolutionised fishing for predatory fish just as angling for carp was revolutionised by the use of boilies. These rubber lures are found in all colours and sizes. The rubber fish have a flat tail whose main function is to cause twitching movements under water. Twisters, on the other hand, are equipped with one or several strands of ribbon instead of a tail which cause the lure's movements. If you angle with rubber lures you will also be using a jig. A jig is a lead head with a large single hook that is inserted in the rubber lure in such a way that

This zander went for a two-part jointed wobbler.

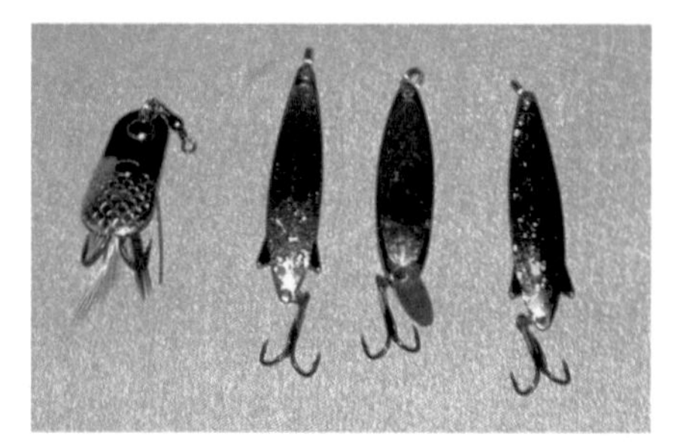

Spoons in different colours and sizes.

the hook protrudes through the centre of the rubber fish's dorsal area. Your choice of jig obviously also determines the size and weight of the lure.

Retrieving the bait is basically the same for all of these kinds of artificial lures, though there are a few differences. Most easily handled are spoons and spinners. For these, all you have to do is cast and then slowly retrieve again. Naturally you can vary the way you retrieve the lure to heighten your success. You can either reel in at varying speeds or occasionally pause the reel-in so the lure can tumble towards the bottom.

Plugs differ enormously in the depths they reach while diving, their shapes, as well as

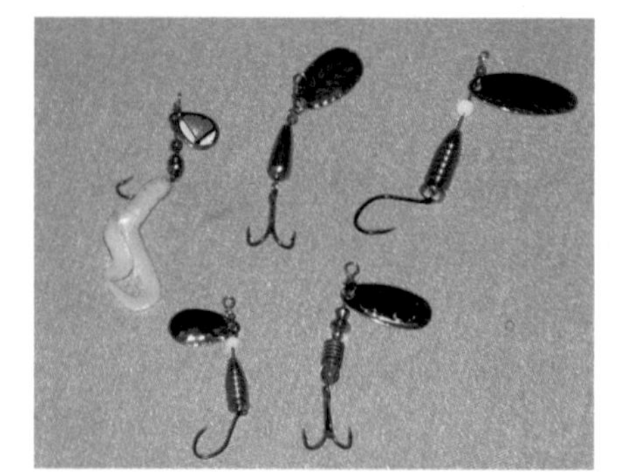

Spinners can be bought in any imaginable colour and variation.

Artificial lures

There are many different kinds of artificial lures used in spin fishing. Spoons and spinners are made of metal, plugs and twisters are made of plastic, and rubber fish and twisters are rubber. If you angle with a rubber fish you will also need a jig, a weighted head attached to a relatively large hook.

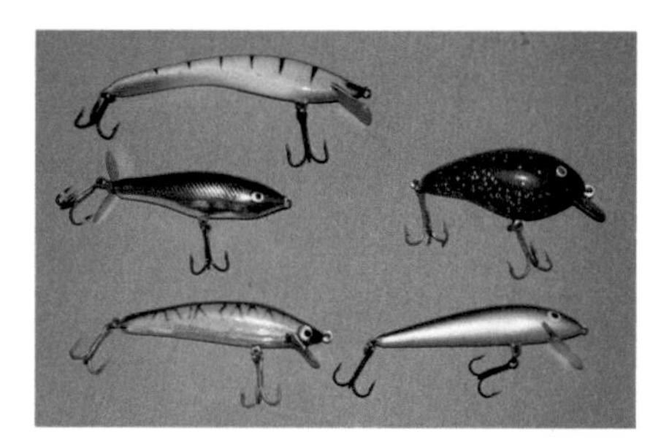

Most plugs are equipped with a diving vane that determines how deep they dive when they are dragged through the water.

their movement patterns under water. Here again, you can be successful by retrieving your lure in a smooth, regular movement, with occasional pauses if you wish. In this case, however, the plugs will rise to the surface during the pauses. You can create very interesting effects by simply twitching the tip of your rod while you retrieve the lure. The sudden changes of direction the lure makes when the rod twitches have attracted the attention of quite a few predatory fish.

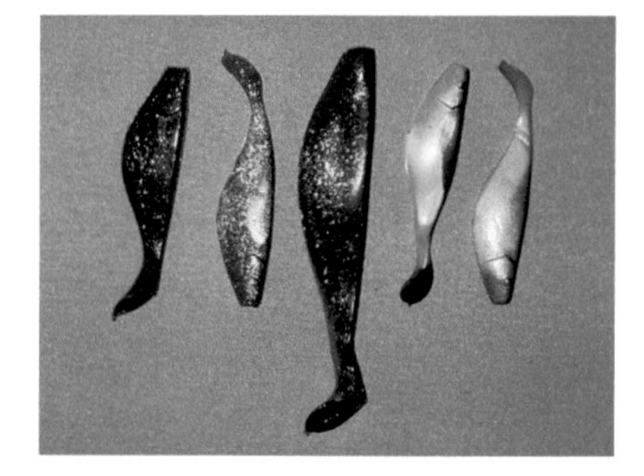

Rubber fish have revolutionised the market in artificial lures.

You will encounter the biggest difference in lure retrieval when fishing with a rubber fish. Although twisters and rubber fish move in specific ways underwater according to their design, you won't achieve maximum success if you simply retrieve in a slow and smooth motion. Instead, try this: cast the lure and let it sink to the bottom with your line slightly taut. The line needs to be taut because the first bite often occurs during this first sinking phase, and a taut line makes it easier to feel when the lure hits the bottom of the water.

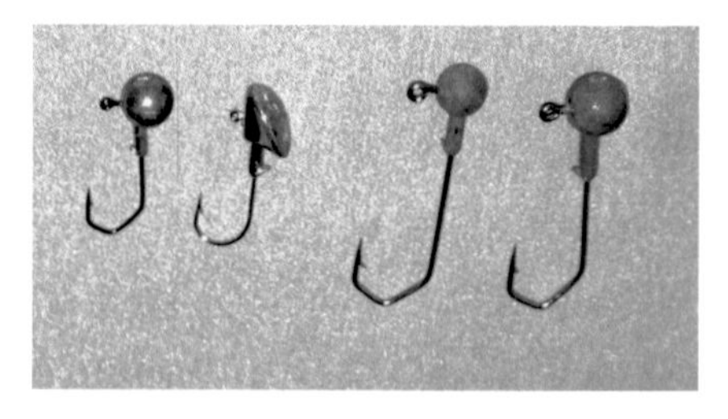

You need to use jigs with rubber fish. These are inserted into the lure in such a way that the hook protrudes from the central dorsal area of the rubber fish.

Now drag the lure across the bottom by lightly lifting the tip of your rod and reeling in

Retrieving the lure

Every artificial lure needs to be cast and then retrieved. You may be successful even if you simply reel in the lure in a regular, smooth movement. More promising, however, are variations in the way you retrieve your bait. This is especially true for rubber fish and twisters which you should cause to "hop" across the bottom of the lake or river.

When you spin fish you can fish along long stretches of shore.

the line. The bait should "hop" little by little from where it lands up to the shore. This is the most successful way to retrieve a rubber lure.

As in all predatory fishing, in most cases you should only spin fish with a steel leader. Unlike other types of predatory fishing, though, ready-made steel leaders of 20 to 40 centimetres may be fully sufficient for spin fishing because the predators don't swallow the entire bait.

This zander could not resist a rubber fish.

Equipment for Fly-Fishing

Playing a fish when fly-fishing is very exciting since you are working with a very sensitive line.

Do you know the movie, *A River Runs Through It*? If not, you should definitely try to see it! When I saw this film for the first time, I knew why fly-fishing is considered the most noble kind of fishing, comparable even to hunting. Ever since then, I have pictured myself standing with my fly rod in every little brook I pass in my car. If you have seen the movie you know what I'm talking about. And believe me: with a little bit of practice and self-confidence, fly-fishing is not so terribly difficult.

If you do plan to start out with fly-fishing, the general-purpose equipment I have suggested above is hardly going to help you. Fly-fishing and the other kinds of angling are as little comparable as the proverbial apples and oranges. You will definitely need a different fishing rod, a different line and a different reel, but you will be able to use all the other tackle.

Let's talk about the fishing rod and fly-fishing line first. Moreso than in other types of fishing, the two are closely intertwined. The fly fisherman's bait (the fly) has almost no weight, yet weight is essential for good casting. The weight therefore has to come from the line itself. This is achieved through the use of various materials to make the line heavier. Clearly, the line and the rod must be in accordance—in this respect fly-fishing is no different from regular angling.

For regular rods, the casting weight indicates how heavy the rigging may be. For fly-fishing, however, the rod classes are made to conform with line-strength categories. Before you buy a fly-fishing rod, you will need to get acquainted with the AFTMA table. AFTMA is an acronym that stands for the American Fishing Tackle Manufacturers Association (an association of companies that produce tackle and equipment). AFTMA developed a classification system for line strength that is used almost everywhere in the world today. The classes are differentiated by number according to the following system: the lower the class number, the lighter and more supple the line.

Fly-fishing rods are rated according to the line strength they are designed to work with. This means that a six-weight rod is designed to work optimally with six-weight line. A two-weight fly-fishing rod with a very fine line can be used to fish in the smallest brooks and runs for trout and grayfish. A ten-weight rod is meant to fish for heavy salmon, while a 15-weight is strong enough to hunt marlin in the Caribbean. Obviously, the higher classes are designed as two-handed rods. For a beginner, I would suggest buying a six-weight rod. This rod can cope with just about any fishing conditions you might encounter in normal European waters.

Let's move on to the reel. The fly-fishing rod is not only much lighter than a regular one, but its reel holder is also at an entirely different spot. The reel is mounted at the very base of the rod, right behind the grips. Fly-fishing reels have a specific design that is actually less complicated than

Equipment for fly-fishing

If you want to try your hand at fly-fishing you will need quite a lot of extra tackle, including a fly-fishing rod, line and reel. It is important that the line and rod are chosen to go together. That is why lines and rods are classified to follow the AFTMA tables. A beginner should start out with a six-weight rod and line.

An idyllic landscape: this is what fly-fishing should be like!

reels for other types of fishing. Inside the casing, the spool sits directly on the axis. This means that the spool is not positioned at an angle to the line, but is aligned with it. A crank on the spool ensures that you can retrieve your lure after casting. At the rear of the casing is a drag control, which applies direct pressure onto the spool and thus resists the pull of the line.

The reel is mounted at the very end of the fly-fishing rod, just below the handle.

High quality fly-fishing reels are mostly made of aluminium, with some less expensive models available in plastic. In recent years, large diameter drum core reels have become increasingly popular. In these models the core, the part on which the line is stored, is larger, which of course means you reel in more line with each turn of the crank. I would suggest you buy a plastic reel with a large diameter core—but if you find such a reel too costly, a regular plastic fly-fishing reel will serve you just fine.

Two fly-fishing reels: on the left a regular reel with line, on the right a large diameter core reel without line.

The only thing piece of basic fly-fishing tackle you're still missing now is the fly. But to make a sensible decision about which of the myriad kinds of flies to select, you need to know something about fly-fishing tactics. So I will talk about casting first, and then about flies.

Different rods—different lines. Rods and lines are divided into various classes according to their relative strength.

Casting and the Right Kind of Fly

Casting is certainly the element that makes fly-fishing unique, and casting gives it its unique aesthetic appeal. I'm sure this is why many people believe that casting must be incredibly complicated—and indeed, it is not the easiest thing. To begin with, though, it will be quite sufficient if you learn how to do an overhead cast. There are a remarkable number of different kinds of cast, but I will present only two of them: the overhead cast, which I will explain in more detail below, and the roll cast.

Casting is what gives fly-fishing its great aesthetic appeal.

Let's start with the overhead cast. This cast is the most fundamental and widely-used by fly-fishermen and fisherwomen. It is used whenever the angler has enough space in front and behind them to make a full sweep. This requires a lot of space because the line is swept back and forth above the angler's head until it is long enough to reach the casting distance the fisherman has in mind. Since beginners should avoid bushes and other obstacles anyway, this should be the first casting technique you try to master upon taking up this hobby.

Grayfish are one of the typical quarry for fly-fishing anglers.

Fly-fishing anglers systematically fish entire sections of a river.

The cast is divided into three phases: the back cast, the extension phase, and the forward cast. In order to understand these phases you have to imagine yourself on the face of a watch. Your head is at 12 o'clock, your back faces 3 o'clock, the soles of your feet are at 6 o'clock and your stomach faces 9 o'clock. Before you cast the line you put out several metres of line into the water. Now start with the back cast. Swing the rod from the nine-o'clock position upwards so that it reaches approximately the twelve-o'clock position. This lifts the line out of the water.

During the extension phase you must wait until the line has stretched out and flown all the way to your back. This phase is very important because if you start the forward cast prematurely the line can come down like a whiplash and hurt the back of your neck or your ears.

Now you begin the forward cast. Once the line is extended nicely all the way behind you, swing the rod forward and the line will fly beautifully straight ahead. This move is repeated as often as necessary to reach your desired casting length. The length of your cast therefore depends on the amount of line you keep in the air. Don't try to extend the line faster by swinging with too much force. The only thing you will achieve with this is making your arms ache a whole lot sooner. If you aim for a simple, supple wrist movement you will usually reach your goal faster than with force.

I won't describe the roll cast in great detail because you will have a much easier time learning this cast once you master the overhead cast. The roll cast is used when there isn't enough space behind the angler to extend the line fully. Lift the tip of your rod approximately to the eleven o'clock position and then bring it with a jerk into the nine-o'clock position. This causes the line to form a circle that rolls across the water surface and then stretches out in front of you. The rolling movement of the line gave this cast its distinctive name.

I must repeat that casting for fly-fishing is not particularly easy. But it is worth investing some time in practicing these techniques. When you do finally join the ranks of those anglers who can keep 20 metres of line flying above their heads, it will be an exhilarating experience. Perhaps the most effective way to learn is with the help of fly-fishing schools. Take the time to get check them out properly first, because some of these schools charge enormous fees. Look for small groups and experienced instructors.

Casting

You certainly don't have to master all the various casts that exist in fly-fishing. I suggest that at the start you work on mastering the overhead cast. Once you have a good grasp on that, you'll find it easier to learn the roll cast or the many other casts used by fly-fishing anglers.

The range of lures lumped together under the heading "flies" includes much more than just flies, and certainly does not include traditional houseflies. Rather, this term describes imitations of fully grown insects, called dry flies; imitations of insect larvae, called nymphs; and also imitation fish that are known as streamers.

Dry flies are always used where trout and other fish feed on insects on or close to the water surface. And that, of course, means you will have to take a closer look at the water you're fishing. Watching the water is an integral part of fly-fishing, because you need to decide not only if you want to fish with a dry fly (or a nymph), but also which kind of fly. In addition, you will have to figure out where the trout are feeding and determine exactly where the water currents are. Taken together, all these pieces of information let you determine the best spot to serve which fly.

The water temperature is still quite low in spring, and only a few insects hatch from eggs during this time. Ephemera such as may flies tend to hatch on warmer days in the heat of midday. Thus it makes sense to fish with imitations of ephemerids

This is a streamer for trout and chub.

during springtime. The more closely your lure resembles the actual insect, the more certain your success.

During the hot summer, insects tend to hatch nearer to the evening hours when it is cooler. The main species now are caddis flies, which accordingly have to be imitated in the lures. As autumn approaches, the insects increasingly revert to hatching around noon again. Caddis flies are still quite frequent during this season, but imitations of stoneflies will also attract trout to your hook.

The trout's main quarry, however, is not fully developed insects, but insect larvae and water scud. In order to imitate these kinds of quarry, you will want to use nymphs. Nymphs are close imitations of insect larvae that are offered to the fish close to the bottom of the water. You can achieve this either by using a sinking rig or by weighting the fly itself. The fly can be weighted either by attaching a little gold head directly to the fly or with the help of split shot threaded onto the leader.

A variety of flies and streamers.

The third category of fly is fish imitations which are called streamers. At a certain age and size, trout start to become predatory fish. These trout feed almost exclusively on other fish. In order to imitate their quarry, you will use streamers. Let the streamer sink to the bottom after casting the line and then bring it back to the shore by "plucking" it forward. That sounds somehow like spin fishing, you say? It does, indeed! Many fly anglers manage to catch zander and pike with streamers as lures. Nowadays, any fisherman or fisherwoman who specialises in spin fishing carries a few streamers in their tackle box. Yes, you did read that correctly: anglers use streamers for spin fishing on spin fishing rods and are quite successful with them!

Flies

The bait used in fly-fishing imitates the small organisms commonly eaten by the angler's intended quarry. They are called flies, a broad term that includes fully developed insects, insect larvae and imitations of small fish. People even use imitations of water scud or locusts as bait. The streamer, a fish imitation, is also used in spin fishing and can be cast on regular spin rigs and rods.

A zander on a fly rod. Trout are not the only ones that can be deceived by flies.

The Bite and Setting the Hook

In the foregoing chapters I have outlined what equipment you need, which bait you should use and where you can find the fish. You are now well prepared for your first fishing trip. The next question is what you should do when a fish actually bites. One thing is for certain: you'll be very excited!

Most fish are extremely cautious when they eat their food. You, the angler, will notice little more than that something is investigating your bait. The tip of your rod vibrates a little, the float bobs some on the water surface, or the bite indicator on your line rises a few millimetres to sink again shortly afterwards. The challenge is for you to find the right moment to set the hook.

As soon as you notice your float twitching on the water, pick up your rod cautiously and take it in your hand. Keep the rod positioned with its tip pointing slightly toward the water. Ideally, your float will start wandering a little across the surface and then disappear suddenly under the water. This is the moment when you must set the hook. Lift the rod quickly, but sensitively, upwards. With this action you are lodging the hook in the mouth of the fish. During the movement of the rod you should be able to feel the weight clearly in the line.

But you will have to keep an eye on something else. When you are fishing with a float, the line will develop a curve after a while. This happens under the influence of the wind and the current and it means that the line will lie on the water in the shape of a bow. Before you try to set the hook you will have to reel in the line far enough to make the bow disappear. Otherwise raising your rod will have no effect, because the movement will simply straighten out the curve in the line. But beware: reeling in the line at this moment must be done with extreme caution in order to avoid alerting the fish being tempted by your bait.

Obviously, no book can tell you what to do in every possi-

The rod is bent, the hook successfully set—right the first time.

Setting the hook when float fishing

The right time to set the hook when float fishing is the moment the float disappears under the water. Other times the float will just travel along the surface—if it continues, set the hook! There are many other situations you will have to experience for yourself, making your own discoveries about what works best.

Waiting for the bite—everything must be within reach.

ble situation. A classic example is the brief disappearance of the float under the surface. By the time you have the rod in your hand, the float is back up. Rather than trying to set the hook, in this case it is better simply to wait. Typically, nothing more will happen and you will decide to put down the rod again and drop back into your chair. But guess what—the instant you are comfortable again, the game will invariably start up anew. I cannot give you any reliable tips for this kind of situation, which I have experienced hundreds of times myself. There is simply no substitute for gaining personal experience and ultimately developing your own intuitive response.

When the bite indicator keeps rising, it is time to set the hook.

When legering, the right moment to set the hook depends on the circumstances. When you fish for non-predatory fish, the tip of the rod serves as your bite indicator. This works best with a leger rod because its tip is very sensitive. The way you set the hook is no different from the technique you use when angling with a float. As soon as you notice the tip of the rod show light action, pick up your rod and hold it as described for fishing with a float. If the tip of the rod continues to move, this is the moment to set the hook.

If you fish with a bite indicator hanging from your line, however, you have to proceed in a slightly different way. Ideally the rod should lie horizontally on two rod rests. As soon as you notice the bite indicator hanging from the line is moving, put your hand on the rod without removing it from the rests (otherwise you will lose the indicator showing you what is happening). Now keep your eyes on the bite indicator. As soon as it starts to rise continually upwards, it's time to set the hook.

Legering for predatory fish, however, is a special case. Typically, zander and pike start by simply picking up the bait, and then they swim off a little way. Only then do these predators start swallowing their prey. So when you fish for predatory fish and notice that the line is running off, you will have to wait a little while. Usually, there will be a short pause during which the line stops running from the reel. Then it will start running off again, and it is time for you to set the hook.

This barbel was landed safely—the hook must have been set at the right moment.

Setting the hook when legering

When legering, the right time to set the hook depends very much on what you are fishing for. If you're trying to catch predatory fish you should wait for the line to run off a second time. When angling for non-predatory fish, set the hook as soon as the rod shows continuous action.

Make sure you always keep in mind how far out you cast the rig. It makes an enormous difference whether you cast your line 5 or 50 metres over the water. If you try to set the hook with a strong jerk when fishing close by, the whole rig can easily whiplash into your face. Yet the same amount of force when your rig is 50 metres out can easily be too little. Generally speaking, the farther away your rig, the more strongly you will have to jerk the rod to set the hook.

When you are spin fishing, remember that predatory fish typically bite with a strong, jerking movement. This can be recognised by an emphatic pull on the rod. In this case it is quite easy to set the hook. But there are other situations when you will only detect a nibble or a slump in the line. If you become aware of this, you should set the hook. Too often, this slump will turn out to be a simple snagging in herbaceous plants, but occasionally it is indeed a cautiously investigative predatory fish that would otherwise have escaped you.

Setting the hook when spin fishing

When spin fishing, react to every nibble you feel by lifting the rod and setting the hook. In most cases the "nibble" will turn out to be caused by the rig getting caught in vegetation, but it would be annoying to lose a fish genuinely on the bite—and, naturally, that one would have been a monster!

Playing the Fish

Keep in mind that water is the natural environment for every fish. This means that it is entirely normal for it to swim through the vegetation, look for food and feed. Then one day, in a split second, everything will change for it because this fish, going about its usual routine, suddenly finds itself hooked to your rig. It is only natural that it will react by putting up the strongest possible resistance. You need to be prepared for that.

When you have set your hook and seen the fish start to fight at the other end of the line, you need to exhaust it and bring it in towards the shore. This is called playing the fish. Naturally, the best way to do this differs from fish to fish. That is one reason I suggest you should gain your first experience with a roach before you go for giants like pike or carp. This is because fish like roach or other grayfish are relatively easy to play. If you happen to have a large fish on your hook you will notice an immense difference. A large carp that finds itself hooked will use all its energy to try and evade its fate. Resistance like that can rightfully be considered a fight.

It is vital to stay calm while playing the fish. Stress and impatience have spelled freedom for many a fish!

If you see that the fish is taking off too much line you must tighten up the drag on your line a little.

The first and most important rule when playing a large fish is to stay calm. The ability, patience and stamina of the angler must all work together. Of course, you will be highly excited and this can cause feverish activity. But you must force yourself to put tension and stress aside and play the fish in complete calm.

Apart from you as the angler, three aspects of your tackle's performance will be vital now. The first is the action of your rod, the second is the flexibility of your line, and the third is the drag control. If these three components work well together, little can go wrong. Make sure that your rod is held upright, in the twelve o'clock position, because only then can you get the full benefit of its action. Naturally, the drag control has

The drag control is screeching, but the fish has already surfaced once.

to be set correctly at the same time, and it may need to be adjusted while you play the fish. All this will become easier as you accumulate practice and experience.

In the best possible scenario, you allow the fish to use up its reserves of energy out in the open water and then bring it in close to the shore. However, there are often obstacles that prevent this. These may include a field of water lilies, for example, a sunken tree, a scour or underwater hill, or perhaps a buoy. The fish know these obstacles and will direct all their efforts to reach safety. You, on the other hand, should do everything possible to prevent that. The fish that reaches the patch of water lilies, for example, is almost always lost to you. So if you realise that your quarry is making for an obstacle, you will have to increase the pressure on it until it changes direction. Of course, you may also lose a fish by doing this—but, then, if the fish succeeds in reaching the obstacle, that loss becomes a virtual certainty. Once the fish starts getting tired you will feel its fight diminishing. Now is the time to start reeling it in evenly, bringing it close to the shore to be landed.

Playing the fish

For many fishermen and fisherwomen, playing the fish is the essence of the sport. This makes perfect sense because it is during play that the angler and the fish pit themselves against each other and compare their wits and strength. Ability, stamina and calm are necessary to win the game. Always take it gently—hasten slowly!

You must remain cool while playing the fish to successfully land a monster like this.

Landing the Fish

The net has to securely land the fish.

Let me begin this section by reiterating my previous comments about the landing net. Do not try to economise when you buy this piece of equipment. Purchase a net whose sides are at least 60 centimetres long—in fact, for modern carp fishing side lengths of more than a metre are quite common. Even if you only aim to catch a rather small roach you can still end up hooking a large carp, and if you should succeed in playing this great fish in spite of your thin line and bring it close to shore—it would be all the more frustrating not to be able to land it because your net was too small.

But let's talk about the landing. By this time, you have exhausted the fish and brought it in close to the shore. Now is the moment to use one hand to put the net in the water. It is a good idea at this point to release the drag control somewhat. Many fish discover new reserves of energy when they see the net. Since the short bit of line still in the water is no longer very flexible, the hook can easily be pulled out or the rig ripped off at this stage. Therefore, it is advisable to keep a light setting on the drag control when the fish is close to the shore.

Push the mouth of the net as far as possible underwater and wait for the net to sink to the bottom. If the net is already in the water it will sink more readily than if it is dry, so I suggest that you keep your

This fish is caught safely in the net.

A landed fish with the hook still in its mouth and a regurgitated piece of bait.

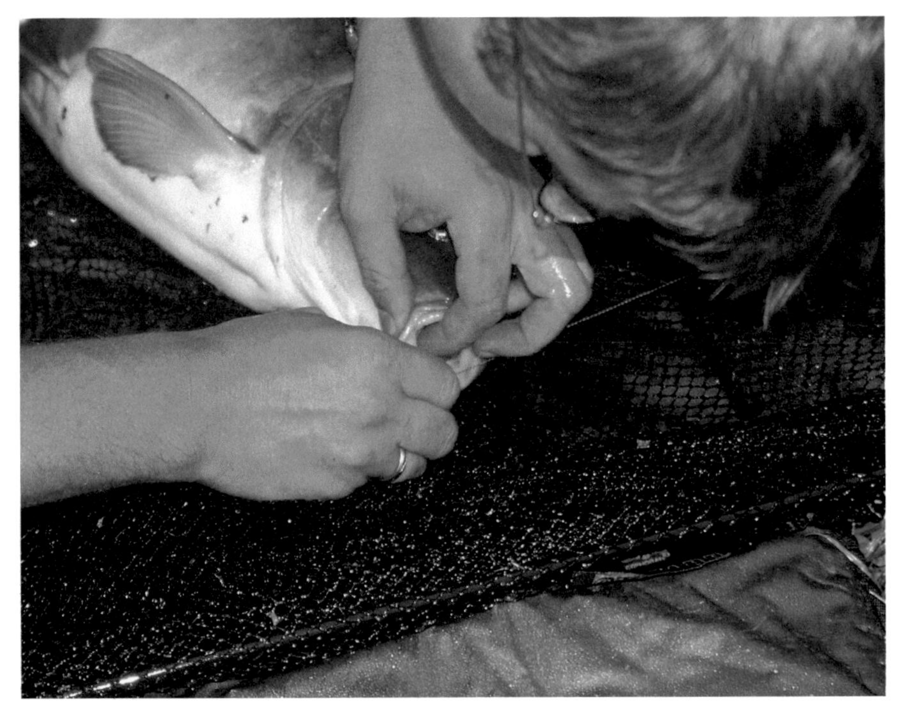

If you return the fish to the water, the hook must be removed with great care.

The landing

The most important rule to observe when landing a fish is never chase after the fish with the net, but always position the fish above the net. Only then should you lift the landing net so that its mesh envelops the fish.

net in the water while you angle. As soon as the net is in the right position, hold it steadily and lead the fish over the net. Be careful: do not be tempted to hunt the fish with the net. This will certainly fail! Always move the fish over the net and not the net under the fish. Once the fish is positioned above the net, lift the net quickly and the mesh will envelop the creature's body.

Now carry the net with the fish ashore. Do not merely grip the handle of the net, but pull it to shore and then lift the net out of the water onto dry land by holding on to the part where the handle connects to the net.

Now you must decide if it is sensible or desirable to keep your prey, or whether you should put it back in the water. Always place the fish on an unhooking mat if possible, because otherwise it could be badly hurt. If you plan to return the fish to the water you will have to remove the hook with particular care and release the fish back into the water with equal care and attention. Always keep your hands wet while doing this to avoid destroying the mucous membrane on the fish's body.

When releasing the fish back to the water, hold it upright until you are sure that it is able to swim again.

Pursuing the Fish on a Boat

People aboard fishing boats should have good sea legs or, at least have anti-seasickness medicine on hand.

In an earlier chapter I mentioned small private trout lakes as being perfect waters for beginners. This should warn you that the sea is certainly not the best water body for a novice angler. But at some point, perhaps, you may fish on the ocean. This is a wonderful thing to do during a vacation, or maybe you live close to the sea. Is there an angler alive who can bear to watch from the sidelines as others catch fish while he or she merely strolls along the harbour? No, on the Atlantic, the North and Baltic Seas, and on the Mediterranean, daily fishing trips are on offer (primarily for tourists) and such a trip can make a vacation near the ocean a really memorable one.

To get off to a good start with saltwater fishing I strongly suggest that you set out on a fishing trawler. These fishing trips are offered in every town along the coasts and they have several advantages. Firstly, you can borrow equipment on the trawler and won't have to buy tackle for your first saltwater fishing trip. Secondly, the experienced crews on these boats will be able to explain everything to you. In addition, the trawler captains are professionals with a great deal of experience, so that nearly every trip will come up with a catch. Codfish is certainly the quarry of choice for the saltwater fishing novice because a codfish hunt so rarely leaves an angler empty-handed.

To begin with, I will explain the tackle necessary for pirking. The term pirking derives from the most important artificial bait for codfish, the pirk. The pirk can is comparable to the spoon in freshwater. Pirks are much slimmer than spoons, but they weigh a good deal more. Light pirks weigh around 50 grammes, while heavy pirks can have weights of up to 200 grammes. Pirks come in all colours, of course.

The rods for pirking are usually about three metres long, but they range between

The tackle for pirking

Angling in saltwater requires different tackle than freshwater fishing. Most importantly, you have to be sure everything is saltwater resistant. I suggest borrowing the tackle for your first saltwater fishing trip. If you decide to go saltwater fishing more often after your first taste of it then you can go out and buy the equipment. Be sure to get sound advice before buying saltwater tackle.

2.70 and 3.60 metres. My personal suggestion would be to use one of the longer models because you can cast farther with a longer rod. On the other hand, your first rod can hardly be too short, since fishing on solid ground is very different to suddenly fishing on a rocking boat full of people. Handling a long rod under these circumstances is a real challenge.

The reel you use for saltwater angling should be strong and saltwater resistant. Apart from that, the spool must be big enough to hold approximately 200 metres of mono line. You don't necessarily need a multiplier reel—a strong fixed-spool reel will suffice and will save you having to make yet another readjustment.

For this kind of angling, I also suggest monofilament line, but you will need a line of at least 0.40 millimetres that has a highly visible colour. Saltwater line is typically available in yellow, red or green. These colours not only make it easier for you but also for the guy or gal next to you on the trawler to see where your line runs into the water. Your remaining tackle must also be saltwaterproof. This is especially true for crims, swivels and treble hooks.

Codfish pirking has a split season, and the fish can be found at different depths at various times of the year. In spring and autumn you will most likely find the fish at depths of 8 to 15 metres, while in summer and winter the pirks have to be lowered as far as 20 to 30 metres. These varying depths obviously affect the weight of your bait. You can reach depths of 8 to 15 metres with pirks weighing between 50 and 100 grammes. If you need to go deeper, your bait should weigh between 120 and 180 grammes.

The trawler captains usually try to afford each of their guests similar opportunities to catch fish. That is why the boat is turned around at the

Codfish and pollock are frequent catches when fishing on the ocean.

An enormous codfish like this is indeed exceptional.

Pirking from a trawler

A trawler is just the right place for your first saltwater fishing trip. An experienced captain will bring you right to the fish and the crew will be happy to answer any of your questions. This is, without doubt, the perfect introduction to saltwater angling.

fishing spot after a while, giving every angler the chance to fish leeward and windward. Leeward (the sheltered side) allows the bait to drift away from the boat. On this side it is best simply to drop the bait off the side of the boat and let the current carry it away. If you are windward, the pirk will at some point drift underneath the boat, which is why the bait is cast out some distance on this side. Fishing on the windward usually brings in more fish than on the lee, since the bait sinks to the necessary angling depth rather than drifting downstream.

The third possible angling situation is when the trawler simply drifts towards the codfish. In this case you want to cast as far as possible, since the approach of the boat's large shadow tends to scare away the fish.

In all three situations the pirk should be dragged somewhere near the bottom of the sea. You should definitely make the bait move in some fashion, which you can achieve by making simple movements with the tip of your rod. On the windward you can move the bait by stopping the line occasionally, which causes the pirk to pause, and then giving more line again.

Apart from the pirk, people fish with several other rigs attached as side-arms to the main line. These rigs have various hooks and baits to attract different kinds of fish. Particularly when you are just starting out, it is better to stick with pirks or (and at most) with one additional

The pollock is an extremely tasty fish!

hook. If you do use a second hook, a red or black twister is a good choice.

When you have successfully hooked your fish, you now have to pump it up to the surface. This involves raising the rod and then lowering it again. As you lower the rod, reel in the line. In this way you will haul in the line, little by little, until the fish finally reaches the surface. Smaller codfish can be hoisted aboard on the line, while the larger ones are landed on board with a special hook, called a gaff. On a typical trawler, you simply have to call for the gaff and a crew member will appear to lend you a hand.

I know you are eager to be on your way. But there are still a few things you should think about before you board the trawler:

1. As a precaution, take some medication to prevent seasickness.

2. Wear weatherproof clothing. The wind over open water is always stronger than it seems to be in the harbour.

3. Keep an eye on your angling colleagues. On board it is often crowded, and lines can easily become tangled. But it is even worse if you accidentally hook one of the other

Big fish in the Mediterranean

Huge mackerel off the coasts of Spain, blue-fin tuna near Italy, and with a little bit of luck even a swordfish—all this and more can be caught in the Mediterranean. However, it is not a good idea to go looking for such enormous fish when you first begin saltwater angling. Once you get going, though, you may well end up trying for one of these giants of the seas.

Fishing for mackerel from a trawler is very popular.

fishermen or fisherwomen when you are trying to cast.

4. You may begin angling only after the horn has blown and you must finish the minute the signal is given.

Mackerel trawlers operate in a very similar way to codfish expeditions. You will use a paternoster rig to catch mackerel. Paternoster rigs have four to six hooks. These hooks are baited with colourful feathers and are attached to side leaders. These colourful rigs are a big attraction for the mackerel. If the captain finds a whole shoal of mackerel it is not uncommon to pull out several fish on one line.

You can hunt for really big game fish in the Mediterranean. Along the Spanish coast there are some enormous species of mackerel and—with luck—swordfish, too. You only have the opportunity to catch a swordfish between June and August, and even then you will need a lot of luck. In Italy you can land the huge blue-fin tuna, which can reach weights of up to 300 kilogrammes. As thrilling as that may be, I strongly counsel you to measure your skill first on codfish and such. These will offer you the perfect introduction to saltwater angling.

With a trailing line in the Mediterranean

If you are a beginner trying to fish in the Mediterranean you should start out with the technique used locally: try angling with a trailing line. In this technique the hook is tied directly onto the end of the main line. In addition you can add side-arms with leaders and hooks as in the paternoster system. As the name indicates, you just let the hooks and bait trail in the current. In this way you can catch fish that swim close to the water surface. Among these are sea bream, sea grayfish and sea bass.

The trip on a trawler is idyllic, at least on the way out to the angling grounds and back to the harbour. In between times, there is a lot of commotion. But maybe this is what makes it such fun...

Surf Fishing and Coast Fishing

Typically, it is a vacation on the beach that makes you a surf angler—or, of course, living somewhere close to the shore. During your evening stroll with the family you can see them everywhere: the surf anglers. Their long rods pointing high towards the sky, some of the fishermen are busy playing their prey. Naturally, this awakens the desire to try it for yourself. It should be possible to combine the two, shouldn't it, the family vacation and some fishing? Many devoted anglers return to the coast as early as the autumn, this time for the express purpose of fishing.

For surf angling you need very sturdy equipment. This is partly owing to the fact that you will have to be able to cast your rig over 80 to 140 metres. In order to achieve this you need special shore rods that are 3.90 to 4.20 metres long. The casting weight of these rods is typically between 100 and 250 grammes. These rods are double-handed, meaning the grip is long enough to be taken into both hands. In order to cast over such long distances these rods have strong through-action. Nonetheless, the tips of these shore rods are very sensitive, so it is still quite easy to recognise a bite. For rod rests, I recommend using only sturdy tripods—these are the only ones that can cope with any situation.

Surf rods at sundown. The best time for bites is just about to begin.

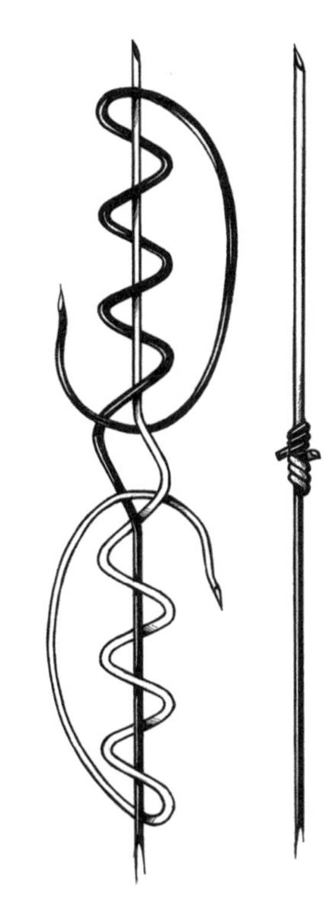

The safest way to link two lines: the double uni-knot.

As far as the reel is concerned, I suggest you use a strong, sturdy, fixed-spool reel. It should hold about 200 metres of 0.40 millimetre line. The line itself should be a monofilament line and have a diameter of 0.35 millimetres.

In order to cast the rig 100 metres and more you will need heavy weights that put a lot of strain on the line. For this reason you will have to use a shock leader, also a monofilament line, but with a diameter of 0.60 millimetres. The length of the shock leader is somewhere between 6 and 8 metres. It is important to reel

Tackle for surfcasting

For surfcasting you need heavy tackle. You will want to use rods with a casting weight of 100 to 250 grammes and a length of 3.90 to 4.20 metres. The sinkers have a weight of between 140 and 250 grammes, depending on weather conditions. Because of the weight of the sinkers, a shock line is essential. The shock line should have a diameter of 0.60 millimetres. Use only tripod rod stands because these will hold your equipment firmly in place.

a few metres of the shock leader onto your spool before casting. The main line and the shock leader are tied together with the double uni-knot. This knot is the best way to join two lines and you will find a diagramme showing how it is tied on page 91.

The sinker needs to weigh at least 140 grammes. If the wind blows strongly towards the land you should use heavier weights of up to 250 grammes. The sinker is attached to the end of the shock line with a strong snap swivel which is saltwater resistant. You can buy these pear-shaped sinkers in many tackle shops or through the internet.

If the currents are strong, I would suggest you use a breakaway. Breakaways settle into the bottom and thus keep your rig securely in place wherever you cast it. Above the sinker you will attach two sidelines, called snoods. In freshwater fishing these would be called leaders. These snoods are, like the freshwater leaders, 0.5 millimetres thinner than the main line, which here means 0.30 millimetres. Attach a size 2 to 1/0 hook to the end of each snood. Sometimes, depending on the water you're fishing, you will need to mount a couple of coloured beads on the snoods. Ask local anglers what they use. If the sea is

Codfish are often caught when surfcasting.

calm, you can use snoods with a length of approximately one metre, if it is rough, they will need to be shorter, say, approximately 35 to 40 centimetres in length.

Without question, the best bait for surfcasting is the lugworm. You can collect lugworms on the coast or buy them in bait and tackle stores. To prevent the lugworms from falling off the hook in the strain of the long casts, attach them to the hook with a long thin bait needle. Clamworms are also occasionally used as bait.

The primary catch for surfcasters is various species of plaice and codfish. Rougher seas or the period after a strong wind has died down create excellent conditions for surf fishing. The best biting times are at dawn and dusk, so be sure to bring along a headlamp. When deciding where to fish, look for places with a variety of seabed features. That is where you cast your bait—as far as you possibly can. Then brace your rod in the tripod, so that the tip points as far upwards as possible. Next pull the line tight until you can feel the sinker drag across the bottom. This way you keep large portions of the line out of the water and thus decrease the pressure of the waves on the line.

A successful day's angling on the shore. This fisherman will go home satisfied indeed.

When a fish strikes, you will see the tip of the rod twitch. If it keeps moving, set the hook firmly. The fish must be played quickly and landed promptly so that it doesn't get a chance to find protection behind vegetation or a stone. On the shoreline, you can use the stranding technique to land the fish—that means taking advantage of the movement of the waves to deposit them on the beach.

Wading through the surf and fishing for sea trout is currently gaining in popularity. Wading works best on gravelly or stony ground. For this technique, the angler wades far out into the sea and sets up spin fishing from there. The best baits are slim sea trout spoons or coast wobblers. These baits work well not only for sea trout, but also for codfish and garfish.

Fishing on the coast

It is important that you are able to cast over a distance of 100 metres or more, and that the sea bottom at your fishing spot has a variety of ground features. The best bait is lugworms, which mainly attract species such as flounder and plaice, but also codfish.

Saltwater angling is certainly quite different from freshwater fishing as you may know it from lakes or streams you are familiar with, but fishing in the sea is certain to be a lot of fun! The many thousands of anglers who travel to the sea shore at least once a year for the express purpose of fishing can't all be wrong—can they?

Glossary

Action: bending characteristic of a rod that determines its response speed and sensitivity. Tip-action rods bend at the tip and are fast and sensitive; middle-action rods bend at the middle and are used for general-purpose freshwater fishing; through-action rods bend from the handle and are used for heavy-duty and saltwater fishing.
Artificial bait: Any kind of bait that is made of plastic, metal or wood and thus does not occur naturally.
Bail arm: Part of the reel responsible for the regular reeling in of the line. It is unfolded by hand before casting the line in order to let the line run unimpeded.
Baitfish: Small fish that is used as bait for predatory fish.
Bite indicator: Device that alerts anglers when a fish takes the bait.
Bobber: A float used exclusively for fishing near the surface.
Boilie: A bait and feed made from various kinds of flour and eggs boiled together, hence its name.
Braided line: Angling line that is braided from several strands.
Breakaway sinker: Sinker with metal wires that help to hold the sinker in place.
Capacity of the spool: Indicates the amount of line that fits on a spool; it is stamped on the spool.
Cast: Using the rod to hurl the bait far over the water.
Casting weight: Indicates the maximum weight the rig and bait can have in order to respond to the optimal casting characteristics of a fishing rod.
Chum: Oily fish feed that crumbles on contact with the water to create a rich feeding ground at a spot chosen by the angler.
Crankbait: A type of plug that has a "beak" which controls the depth to which it dives.
Drag control: Part of the reel, used to control the resistance encountered by a fish on the line. Often sits at the end of the reel.
Dry flies: Dry flies imitate various fully developed insects. Unlike the wet fly or nymph the dry fly remains on the water surface.
Eyed hook: All hooks that have an eye through which line can be threaded.
Fathoming: Finding out the depth of the water.
Fathoming rod: Fishing rod that is used not to catch fish but to determine the depth of the water.
Fathoming sinker: Any heavy weight that can be used to find out the depth of water.
Feed ball: Mixed feed to which water is added; can then be rolled into little balls.
Feeding: Regularly putting food into the water at a certain spot to accustom the fish to feeding at that particular fishing spot.
Fishing license or permit: You can get a license after passing a fishing test and in many countries you must have one to be allowed to go fishing.
Fixed-spool reel: A fishing reel with a spool attached at a right angle to the casting direction. It is the most-used fishing reel.
Flexibility of the line: Fishing lines have different degrees of flexibility. Multifilament lines are the least flexible.
Float: Bite indicator that shows when a fish has taken the bait by disappearing under the water surface; it may also support bait at the desired depth.
Float fishing: Angling technique in which a float is used. With this technique the bait can be offered at any desired depth.
Fly-fishing reel: Fishing reel that is adapted to the specific demands of fly-fishing.
Fly-fishing: A specific fishing technique which uses artificial bait called flies.
Forceps: Gripping device used for disengaging the hook from the mouth of the fish.
Front drag: Part of the fishing reel; a drag located at the head of the reel is called a front drag.
Gaff: A device with a metal hook used to land larger fish. It should only be used in particular circumstances, particularly in saltwater fishing.
Ground fishing: see Legering
Jig: A hook with a weighted metal head; the hook can be inserted in all rubber bait.
Landing net: A large-mouthed net for landing the fish. It is important to choose one large enough to land a big predator fish.
Lateral line: A row of pores containing nerve endings along the midline of a fish's body. It extends from gill to tail.
Leader: Line between the hook and the rig. The leader is always somewhat thinner than the main line to create a natural breaking point in case of snags.
Leger rod: A special kind of rod that is made for ground fishing with a swim feeder.
Legering: Fishing technique in which the bait is offered on the bottom of the body of water.
Monofilament line (mono): Fishing line that consists of a single strand, usually nylon.

Multiplier reel: An extremely heavy-duty reel that puts the line directly on the spool with no change in direction.
Night float: Transparent plastic tube filled with chemical substances which form a gas that shines in the dark.
Nymph: Wet fly imitating an insect that is not fully developed. Used in deeper waters.
Particle: All granular bait such as maize, hemp seed or nuts.
Paternoster system: A multiple-hook rig with a separate leader for each hook.
Pirk: Artificial bait that resembles a spoon but is usually slimmer. Used exclusively for saltwater angling.
Playing: The slow exhausting of the fish so that the catch can be landed safely.
Plug: Artificial bait made of wood or plastic that imitates a prey fish and can dive to various depths.
Polywag: Slim float that can only be slipped on the line on one side. Polywags are often equipped with interchangeable weights.
Pop-up rig: Sinker with an additional air-filled plastic tube that stays upright when it reaches the bottom.
Priest: A device used to stun a landed fish before it is killed humanely.
Pump and reel: In deep saltwater fishing, technique of bringing in a fish by repeatedly raising the rod steadily, then lowering briskly while reeling in.
Ready-made leader: A complete leader with hook available for purchase; often with a loop to attach to a snap swivel. They can be bought ready-tied in tackle shops.
Quiver tip: Very sensitive, interchangeable tip of some fishing rods, used as a bite indicator.
Rig: The combination of hook, leader, weight, and possibly also a float whose design varies according to your fishing technique.
Rod action: see Action
Rod rest: Device to prop up and secure the rod while in use.
Rubber fish: Artificial bait that imitates a predator fish's quarry.
Safety rig: A rig for carp fishing in which the weight is attached such that it can slip off the rig if the leader breaks.
Self-hooking rig: A rig designed to cause a fish to flee right after the bite. When the fish flees, it swims against the drag of the weight, thus setting the hook.
Setting the hook: Embedding the hook firmly into a fish's mouth, often by quickly pulling backwards on the rod.
Shock line: A line that is attached to the front end of the main line. It is used above obstacles such as mussel banks to avoid a breaking of the line.
Shore rod: Double-handed, long, heavy rod adapted to the specific conditions of surf casting.
Sinker: A heavy weight that is attached to the leader to pull the bait to the bottom.
Sliding or running weight: A weight with a hole through the middle for the line to run through.
Snap swivel: A swivel with a metal snap on one end, used to attach a rig, leader, or weight.
Snood: A kind of leader that can be used as a flanking leader when fishing in saltwater.
Spade-end hook: Hook that is attached to the line by a flattened part at the top, called the spade.
Spare spool: The main spool is the part of the reel that holds the line. A spare spool can be used to take along a second type of line.
Spin fishing: A very active fishing technique in which predator fish are lured with a variety of artificial baits. Makes it possible to fish large areas of water.
Spinner: An artificial metal bait with a rotating blade.
Split shot: Small round metal weights which are split so they can be threaded onto the line.
Spoon: Spoon-shaped artificial bait made of metal which imitates the prey of a predatory fish.
Streamer: A large, bushy fly which is usually intended to imitate a small sick fish.
Swim feeder: A small basket or other container made of plastic or metal which is filled with feed. It serves to attract fish.
Swingtip: An interchangeable tip of a fishing rod that is used as a bite indicator.
Swivel: A small metal piece with two eyes that rotate freely in order to prevent the line twisting and tangling. It is used to connect the rig to the main line.
Telescopic rod: A fishing rod in which the different parts can be pushed together or extended as in a telescope.
Tripod: A rod rest with three feet that is used to rest the rod securely. Designed especially for shore fishing.
Twister: Rubber fish with a tail.
Two- or three-part rod: Fishing rod consisting of two or three parts which are fitted together.
Unhooking mat: Padded mat on which the fish can be placed securely while the hook is removed from its mouth.
Whiting: A general term for smallish non-predatory fish such as bream and roach.
Wobbler: An artificial bait that shimmers and wobbles in the water to attract predatory fish.

Index